# FROM EXPERT TO EXECUTIVE

FROM

# EXPERT

TO

# EXECUTIVE

MASTERING THE A~~BC~~s OF
LEADING

*SOPs*

*The tale of a bright idea
and the leaders who
embraced it*

# EDWARD E. TYSON

*WITH* MICHAEL ASHLEY

PERSYNERGY PRESS
*DOVE CANYON, CA*
2020

ISBN: 979-8-64379553-7

Any references to historical events, real people, or real places are used fictitiously. Names, characters, and places are products of the author's imagination.

Book design by Claudine Mansour Design

**PerSynergy Press**
*5 Somerset*
*Dove Canyon, CA 92679*

www.LeadershipSOPs.com
www.PerSynergyConsulting.com

*To those who endeavor to accomplish together*
*what they could never do alone.*

# CONTENTS

# INTRODUCTION

Every step on the journey from expert to executive leads away from your craft. This sentiment is easier to grasp than embrace; and neither grasping nor embracing it is a requirement for reaching the rank, responsibilities, or rewards of an executive. As you may know from firsthand experience, many experts successfully climb the career ladder unaware their value to the organization is shifting. With each step, they continue to cling to their technical capabilities, hanging onto the belief that it is the autonomy, scope, and impact of their work (not the work itself) that is changing. These leaders pour their lives into their work, many of them producing outstanding results and widespread accolades.

Meanwhile, under the surface, a dangerous dynamic is unfolding. The more time a leader spends on the team's work (the technical work), the less time they leave for leading. Strategy development and coordination, organizational alignment, coaching, and other responsibilities get pushed aside in favor of solving technical puzzles and doing the tactical work. Additionally, as these leaders "lean in" too hard and too far into the team's work, they can't help but displace or knock into those who are supposed to be doing it. This is often intimidating and awkward for the team. Even when it is welcome, and the team asks for the support, it can result in lower employee engagement and the stagnation of capabilities as the leader continues laying claim to the most interesting and advanced work of the team.

Clearly, the longer this cycle continues, the worse the consequences can be for any organization. However, as employee dissatisfaction grows and team capabilities flatline, these departments become even more dependent on their overzealous executives (because the team is no longer capable of doing the work on its own). This dynamic complicates changing course and reinforces the leader's idea that it is their technical skills the company values most.

Certainly, this is not the case for every expert who accepts the leadership challenge. I do not intend to paint everyone with the same broad brush. Indeed, on the other side of this coin are leaders with technical backgrounds who instantly discover they have entered a vastly different world—a world with a new set of challenges for which their previous studies and experiences have left them unprepared. These leaders often act quickly to seek out resources to help close the knowledge gap and aid in their transformation.

Tragically, it doesn't matter if you are a leader who instantly "gets it" or if you are one who experiences an uncomfortable, midstream "awakening." All paths "lead" to a $360 billion training industrial complex producing a lot of concepts, content, coaches and trainers—but not enough leading.

As an executive coach and consultant, I work with executives every day. Most report being either ill-equipped or too busy to lead. Further, they are not satisfied with the leadership they see occurring above or below them. Likewise, the Global Leadership Forecast 2018, jointly published by DDI, The Conference Board and EY, showed only 14 percent of CEOs surveyed believed they have the leadership talent necessary. Everyone, it seems, is troubled by the amount of time leaders spend leading (versus "doing"), yet the problem persists.

Why aren't we getting a sufficient return on our development dollars? Is the problem that we aren't getting a return at all, or are we simply not getting a lasting return? Are we clear about what we are trying to achieve or measure? What do we mean when we say leaders need to spend more time leading and less time "doing"? Is it possible to measure how much someone leads (can we know if they are doing it more or less)?

These are just a few of the difficult questions preoccupying my mind over the past several years. Since I am a practitioner, I have been investigating these problems introspectively, through my work and with my colleagues (versus through research). Answers came to me slowly at first, then in bunches. In the end, I believe I uncovered a simple truth: our leaders aren't leading because we haven't clearly defined the term or differentiated their work from their team's work. We have allowed leadership to be reduced to competency decks comprised largely of interpersonal skills and leadership styles versus the real work of leading. We don't teach soccer strikers sportsmanship and expect them to understand their position on the field of play. Yet, this is exactly what we do for leaders.

My journey of reflection, trial and error brought me newfound clarity, conviction and results. I spent the past several years packaging these ideas into a simple but surprisingly robust framework (explaining the work of leading and why we do it) and a powerful methodology (detailing the path to personal mastery, enhanced collaboration and effective mentoring).

The balance of this short *Introduction* explores this model by investigating three of the most important insights I had while composing it. The rest of the book, however, takes a completely different approach, wrapping the model in a compelling fictional tale designed to transport you into the minds of several reluctant leaders (from CEOs to supervisors) who use both the framework and methodology to better grasp what leading is and choose it over their areas of expertise.

*INSIGHT #1*
## LEADING IS A PROCESS

I started my small coaching and consulting business after serving in the Marine Corps, earning degrees in philosophy and organizational development, and spending 15 years climbing the corporate ladder. I was very proud of my modest accomplishments. This pride, combined with my need to differentiate my business, drove a burning desire to say my coaching practice was different and better than those to my right and left. Unfortunately, from a process perspective, my practice was completely unremarkable . . . and so were my results. In the near-term, my clients were ecstatic. However, looking across years, I found many struggled to continue their growth, and some even regressed. I was frustrated. Why was I unable to consistently create lasting results? What could I do to help my clients beat the odds? What could I do that was better and different?

As a coach, I administered self and multisource assessments (such as personality tests and 360 degree feedback surveys). I helped my clients consider and set professional development goals. My clients and I created thoughtful action plans focused on reframing limiting thoughts and beliefs, identifying and overcoming knowledge gaps, and experimenting with new behaviors. In short, I was doing what most good executive coaches do . . . but, for some reason, I was expecting "better" results. As a former vice president of process improvement, the irony of this was not lost on me. Yes, doing the same thing again and again (just like everyone else) and expecting a different result is the definition of insanity. We can thank Dr. Einstein for giving this bit of insight to us.

Obviously, if I wanted better and more lasting results, I needed a better process. As I continued to explore this question, my mind kept returning to John Kotter's book, *Leading Change*. I have trouble remembering the details of most leadership models without having them in front of me (which is why my own model leans heavily on simple mnemonic devices), nevertheless, I always seem to remember the failure mode associated with Kotter's eighth step, "NEGLECTING TO ANCHOR CHANGES FIRMLY IN THE CORPORATE CULTURE." This phrase echoed across my mind my entire career.

Of course, Kotter was talking about enterprise-wide change, not transforming the behavior of a single individual. But the more I thought about my dilemma of creating lasting individual change, the more I realized this warning still applied. Culture, while treated as a slippery subject by many, is just the most visible and shared patterns of thinking, speaking, and acting in a group.

Applying this thinking to individuals allowed me to frame my dilemma as an inability to help my clients anchor new insights, language, and behaviors into their existing patterns of thinking, speaking, and acting. It was a simple thought (which no doubt, you already had), but it focused my thinking and helped put me into action. The change with my clients was subtle but important. I started asking them to pursue their development objectives by building, improving and engaging in repeatable processes (with specific triggers and participants). The results were far more tangible, leading to better clarity and follow-through.

For example, an executive at a global technology firm was struggling with delegation and accountability. She was holding onto too much for too long and, when she finally did assign the work to someone else, she was almost always unhappy with the results. Working together, we explored the entire macro-level process involved. We started using one piece of work as an example. She determined which roles on her team were appropriate for that work and assessed the ability of the talent available in those roles to do that specific work function. She then developed people-specific strategies for assigning, executing, monitoring and evaluating the work (based on the skills assessment of each individual). Armed with a better understanding of how her organizational system ought to flow into her capabilities assessments and inform her work assignment and coaching strategies, she was able to spot gaps and build a better, more effective process with clear steps, participants and triggers. Her confidence soared and so did her results.

Then one day, as I was explaining the concept to an energy executive, I blurted out, "Let's talk about your **LeadershipSOPs**." My eyes went wide as I continued, "You know, your standard operating procedures, for leading." Eureka! Somehow, finding the right words created a different level of commitment to the philosophy I had been building. I started thinking about the deeper value of starting and ending with a systems approach to leadership. In fact, I began thinking about leadership itself as an interconnected system of people processes. The list of benefits to this mind-shift was long and seemed to come at me from all sides.

Leaders can leverage **LeadershipSOPs** to:

• Differentiate leadership routines from technical work
• Engage strengths more consistently
• Replace or de-emphasize unwanted behaviors
• Define and routinely express new behaviors
• Increase personal proficiency and feel through repetition
• Foster predictability, trust and collaboration
• Establish a platform for a lifetime of continuous improvement
• Drive a more intentional leadership brand
• Simplify mentoring efforts with more concrete conversations.

As my new insights surrounding the **LeadershipSOPs** continued to build, I was struck by a paradox of sorts. On one hand, the approach was revolutionizing my coaching conversations and results. On the other hand, I couldn't shake the feeling these insights were nothing new. In fact, I could hear the ghost of Stephen Covey, author of *The 7 Habits of Highly Effective People*, insisting he had told me (and millions of his closest friends) about the power of habits 25 plus years earlier. And, of course, there were others. Well before Covey's best-selling book (way back in the 1950s), process and quality improvement innovators such as W. Edwards Deming started introducing the world to the expansive power of process thinking. As it turned out, I was relatively late to the party and just standing on the shoulders of giants.

## INSIGHT #2
## THE MEANS JUSTIFY THE ENDS

Generally, my clients are global experts in senior leadership roles. They are very impressive individuals with high IQs whose unparalleled technical expertise brought them to the tops of their corporations. Working alongside them, it is easy to become inspired by the limitless power of the human mind. Balancing this admiration, though, is an important conclusion that I hope they would grant me the latitude to make artfully and without judgement. Expertise is a thief—it steals your focus and robs your time. For many, this is a known and completely acceptable exchange, making it less a robbery and more a transaction. For others, it comes as quite a surprise when the blinders are lifted, and they reclaim their perspective on the world around them.

Whether by a conscious trade or a thief in the night, a prolonged hyperfocus on technical work brings with it a lack of focus on other things. For some, this manifests itself in poor self-awareness and social skills, as is frequently depicted in the entertainment industry, but I have had just as many clients who did not fit this mold. The common denominator doesn't seem to have anything to do with emotional intelligence or introversion versus extroversion. It seems to me to be a genuine and overwhelming love for and interest in the work. And this love, fueled by superior capabilities and a lifetime of accolades, invariably leads to a reluctance to set it aside.

The most common scenario resulting from this mindset typically leads to defining one's role as representing the highest technical expertise for the subject-matter area. The problem is, if one follows this logic to its conclusion, these leaders are essentially defining their jobs in terms of the end product or service their function provides. In other words, the people are the "means" and the products or services are the "ends." This leads to the obvious prioritization of technical work and work outcomes (on-time, highest quality, lowest cost, etcetera) over more humanistic, sustainable, and proactive measures of success, such as employee engagement, career progression, and team development. In this scenario, the purpose of the role (and therefore leading) is reduced to achieving objectives through others, which in practice looks and feels like, "the ends justify the means."

Of course, as someone trying to engage leaders in leading, it seems obvious to me that leadership is more about the people than the work. Sure, results matter, the budget matters, etcetera; but you just don't get there without your people (or you only get there once and then never again). My clients "seem" to understand this, too. On a certain level, they know from Day One our work is to help them make progress in this area. And yet, time and again, I encounter significant resistance to change because they see their *real* work as synonymous with the team's technical work—leaving them very little time for what I consider leadership and what they subconsciously consider "side work."

Realizing I needed to hit this issue head-on, I amended my elevator speech to "**LeadershipSOPs** are your standard operating procedures for developing your teams." This small change did little to resolve the objection or fix the problem; but it did have an impact. It helped raise this important issue early in our discussions. This, however, had an unexpected side-effect: conflict.

I quickly found my clients' keen minds and practical notions made it difficult to "prove" them wrong about anything. Many accused me of falling for a Pollyanna-ish fairytale. They were steadfastly convinced they were recruited and/or promoted repeatedly because of their technical competence and their ability to direct the work—not to develop a team. Secretly, I feared many of them were right. I suspected they were, in fact, operating within cultures that had produced and reinforced the notions they were sharing. I also suspected it wasn't wise for me to engage too forcefully with my clients while trying to build trust and rapport. On shaky ground, I continued exploring ways to impart the important belief that capability building is core to the purpose of leading and "results" are just one indicator of success in that endeavor.

My best academic argument was, and still is, this: we conceive of leadership when we hold an objective in our minds we cannot achieve alone. We bring it to life when we act to engage others for the purposes of generating the will and capacity to collaborate. Yes, there is an objective, and the objective is an important impetus and success measure, but it cannot be the primary focus of the leader. The leader's role is to create the capacity for goal attainment. By accepting the role, a leader is accepting the responsibility for generating the *means* for goal achievement. The purpose of leading is to create the will and capacity for collaboration, making leadership, at its core, a process of social organization. If there is no need for a group of people to be both willing and capable of collaboration, there is no need for leading.

This is admittedly a nuanced argument; it is not always successful. My most successful tactic (meaning the one that burns the least time and relationship capital) consists of a simple acknowledgement . . . with a caveat. "Perhaps you are right." I say. "In the end, you can't escape accountability for results. You will have a problem on your hands if you develop a powerful team but do not produce any results. However, is it really possible to develop a powerful team that is satisfied with failure? What would you do differently if at least 50 percent of your reason for being (in an organizational sense) were the production of a powerful, willing, and capable team? What people processes would you add to your work processes? What work processes would you withdraw from to create the time?"

Much to my surprise, this approach often sidestepped the unpleasant and somewhat unhelpful debates altogether. Very quickly we turned corners together and I was able to witness the power of brilliant minds refocusing on the will and capabilities of their teams. We were able to jump almost instantly to assessing and developing **LeadershipSOPs**. Boom! Their thinking changed, their language changed, and their actions followed. It was awesome. Shining the bright light of brilliant minds onto *people puzzles* can be quite a powerful thing.

Nearly a year later, while working with Ken Harper (a colleague who previously headed Tesla's leadership program), the language improved a bit more. Ken was helping me translate the **LeadershipSOPs** into a six-month cohort program for executives. We were behind the eight ball. Our strategic partner, Leaderology, sold the program before it was complete (based on a back-of-a-napkin description and a whole lot of trust in Leaderology CEO Marissa Waldman).

The premature but very welcome sales left Ken and me (along with Leaderology's head of content strategy and delivery, Talia Seehoff) scrambling to finish the training design and materials in time. As we huddled inside my mobile office, a Sprinter van customized for on-the-go meetings, Ken uttered the phrase "community of effort." I had never heard the phrase before. He brought it up in reference to a slide we were building on the purpose of organizational design—but as soon as I heard it, I had another "purpose" in mind.

"Community of Effort" felt more expansive and less cliché than "team." It implied ad hoc collaborations, formal and matrixed groups, departments, divisions, and entire organizations. More than that, "community" indicated interdependence and collab-oration—while "effort" put the focus on the "means" versus the "ends." As you may have guessed, I instantly amended my evolving positioning statement to include the term. It now read: **Leader-shipSOPs** are your standard operating procedures for developing your communities of effort."

## INSIGHT #3
# WITH PURPOSE COMES CLARITY

*Leadership is a process of social organization meant to yield willing, ca-pable, and sustainable communities of effort.* Once again, better words had propelled me forward in my journey. Shortly after adopting the "Community of Effort" terminology, I began pressure testing this new definition of leadership. The phrase was exactly what I needed to help me articulate the process and purpose of leading.

Defining leadership and the purpose of leading was much "big-ger" than what I set out to do when I began searching for a more effective coaching process, but as I continued to think about it, I re-alized (once again) I wasn't the first person to have these thoughts. I was simply integrating and clarifying existing thoughts. It would be laughable to suggest I was the first person to bring a humanistic focus to the purpose of leading or to suggest "teaming" is what leaders must do. In fact, it was another massive insight that later seemed like common sense. And yet, I could not deny my clients were responding differently and better than they had before. They were definitively leading more. Our exploration of the topic was bringing them better clarity, creating a common language and de-livering what I had set out to deliver: "more" leading. Innovative or old hat, I was onto something.

Still, my client dialogue was too wide open . . . too limitless. I could see some clients listening to my approach and feeling as if it only gave them enough direction to know they were lost. At first,

I considered this struggle to be part of their leadership journey. I believed each leader needed to have the flexibility to craft solutions that worked for their business and their teams. I rejected the notion that any specific set of **LeadershipSOPs** could possibly apply to every leader in every situation. That said, there was just no denying it—failing to limit the possibilities or at least provide some type of guidance was *limiting* my clients' ability to focus.

Despite my hesitancy, I started collecting my favorite examples as a way to be more concrete and help my clients zero in on strengths, gaps and opportunities. My examples included strategic planning processes, delegation procedures, coaching models, etcetera. In my sessions, I would provide the examples, then ask questions such as, "Do you currently have **LeadershipSOPs** to address these areas? How often do you engage in them? With whom? What tools do you use? What are your results? Should this be a focus area for us? Why or why not?"

Providing the examples helped. They helped a lot. However, two things began to worry me. One, I was talking too much and listening too little—exactly what every coach tries to avoid. Two, I was dismayed by how often, "establishing one-on-ones with direct reports," was specifically making it to the list of new **LeadershipSOPs**. To be clear, I wasn't dismayed because of this idea's elementary nature. I was concerned because if this were a valuable insight, surely there were a lot of other basic gaps we should be exploring more comprehensively. The problem became: how can I cover the bases from A to Z without lecturing versus listening?

There is nothing like a horrendously long drive through the desert to focus an extrovert like me. So, when my best friend and industrial organizational psychologist, Eric Sydell, mentioned he was going to be in Phoenix for a few days, I hopped in my car without much notice. I used the pressure of our pending conversation (and the silence of the eight-hour drive) from Orange County, California, to Phoenix to organize the problem in my head.

I made amazing progress. By the time I arrived in Phoenix, I had reached a new level of clarity. At that point, my **LeadershipSOPs** model defined the purpose of leading (developing communities of effort) and a methodology for doing it (leveraging standard operating procedures) but it lacked a perspective on the actual domains of leading. What specific areas of leadership should my clients explore?

In the harsh silence of that desert drive, the problem and the solution struck me as simple. If the purpose of leading is producing willing and capable communities of effort, these communities must be **created or designed** (by devising or clarifying strategies, cultures, objectives, purposes, ecosystems, work methods, organizational structures, rewards, knowledge and capabilities); they must be **run as intended** (with planning, accountability and stakeholder engagement mechanisms) and **continuously improved** (from an individual, team and organizational perspective).

I brought Eric up-to-date over dinner. He was the first person to hear me awkwardly describe the three domains of leading as structuring, operating, and process improving your communities of effort. For the most part, he reacted enthusiastically. But the problem, of course, was "structure" and "operate" worked really well together regardless of tense; but "process improvement" took two words to say (and just didn't sound right with the other two, no matter how you said it).

I was intent on finding a single word that began with the letter "P" and stood for both performance improvement and process improvement. I was fixated on this solution because using the **LeadershipSOPs** acronym as a double entendre to stand for both standard operating procedures and structure, operate and p-something seemed like too elegant of a solution to pass up. Eric and I put down our forks, picked up our phones, and ran through scores of synonyms. Frustrated, I looked up from my phone and said, "It's too perfect not to work!"

I knew the trip had been worth the torturous drive when Eric reached across the table, smacked me in the arm and said, "That's it—*perfect!*" Cue the fireworks.

| | | | |

***LeadershipSOPs*** *are your standard operating procedures for structuring, operating, and perfecting your communities of effort.*

| | | | |

More than a year later, Ken, Talia, and I were still working out the kinks on the dimensions beneath these three simple domains.

Somehow, amidst the flurry of the busiest year of my life, we did it. The journey and work humbled me. The resulting model took on a meaning and depth well beyond my initial attempts to just differentiate my process in the marketplace. And, I will be forever thankful for the minds that helped sharpen it—those I already mentioned by name, as well as Michael Ashley (who helped me bring the characters to life), Mayssa Attar (who improved my biotech vocabulary), and, of course, Robert Heaton and my wife, Jennifer (both of whom perfect most everything I touch).

To leaders with the interest and know-how to apply this model without much more description, I offer the condensed overview on the following page. To those who would prefer to explore it in more depth before testing it out, I offer the subsequent chapters of this book as a more approachable introduction to how this disruptive, yet remarkably common-sense model can be put to use to help you lead and mentor more . . . and more effectively.

If these ideas should take root in your mind, as they have mine, please join our journey at www.LeadershipSOPs.com. My greatest hope is we can do something together I could not do alone.

# LEADERSHIP SOPs

*Your standard operating procedures for structuring, operating, and perfecting your communities of effort.*

| STRUCTURE | OPERATE | PERFECT |
|---|---|---|
| *SCOPE the WORK* | *Set the PASE* | *Transform & Master* |

### SCOPE

Every community of effort has a SCOPE. It represents the primary business architecture of the group. Reaching beyond mission, vision and values, SCOPE stands for: strategy, culture, objectives, purpose, and ecosystem.

### WORK

The WORK acronym comprises the second half of the LeadershipSOPs organizational design model, alluding to the work methods, organizational structures, rewards and recognition, knowledge and capabilities required to pursue and deliver the SCOPE.

### PASE

The PASE model includes planning (operational and financial), accountability, and stakeholder engagement. Frequently, these operational dimensions account for the bulk of a leader's time.

### AEMEA
#### Accountability Model

The AEMEA accountability model breaks down the "A" in PASE into the critical components of a work execution system with each letter referring to the assignment processes; execution planning; monitoring mechanisms; evaluation routines; and actions required to manage performance.

### ECT(M)

Personal transformation and change leadership are hard. Most (66% or more) change initiatives result in failure. ECT(M) is an individual coaching, team development and organizational transformation model which actively engages those seeking or impacted by change in the proactive phases of what is known as the change curve. The model focuses on cycling through the explore, clarify, and transform phases multiple times until success is ultimately found. Then, the pursuit of mastery begins by integrating the change into new standard operating procedures.

# PRELUDE

*Techular Biologics*

Six years ago, Maaksharth Reddy and Raj Patel founded Techular Biologics with a silent financial partner. The two men, both now 47 years old, had been friends since graduate school. Before starting their company, each had found success in a corner of the pharmaceutical industry commonly referred to as biotech. While Raj was an amazing scientist, Mak, as everyone called him, lived in the more exciting world of ideas. An extrovert by nature, he enjoyed engaging and directing others, pushing them to succeed. And, he was good at it, particularly the pushing part.

Due to Mak's charisma, he rose rapidly through the ranks to take command of an R&D department at a high-profile company. Raj found his success elsewhere, where his scientific skills distinguished him, leading to significant prominence among research scholars but no flashy title.

Though both made names for themselves through very different talents at different companies, they remained in close contact through the years. Mak always had his best ideas standing next to Raj—typically because Raj had mumbled them first—and Raj never felt more connected to the world than when he was with Mak—because being with Mak meant being with an entire entourage. Whenever they would reunite at conferences and life events, Mak would pitch Raj on his latest project he thought they should take up together. Mak was Raj's favorite person and darn near his only friend; but Mak's business ideas were always too commercial and whimsical to interest Raj. Consequently, he always stayed where he was, doing what he loved.

Then tragedy struck. And, as tragedy often does, it changed things. Raj's mother was diagnosed with Alzheimer's and he instantly became obsessed with the disease. His role at the time didn't afford him the ability to pursue pet projects "on the clock," but he began pouring every minute of his spare time into understanding the disease and possible treatments. At the very least, he sought to help the scientific community think differently about the problem that had stumped it for decades. After several years of side research and endless correspondence with scientists around the world, Raj had a high degree of certainty regarding the three most promising areas of inquiry. He knew his theories were sound but none of the scientists he was corresponding with were willing to abandon their own theories (or more importantly their grants) to test his.

Frustrated with his lack of ability to get anyone to listen, Raj turned to Mak for advice. After all, Mak's core competency was getting scientists to see things his way. Mak reviewed Raj's work and immediately realized the science was sound (*How could it not be?* It was Raj). Mak's mind exploded. This was exactly the type of opportunity investors were scrambling for as the baby boomers began dealing with this wretched disease in record numbers. Mak looked into his friend's eyes. Behind the anxiety and frustration, he saw something, something . . . else. Raj had not just discovered a radical new treatment approach. He had also found resolve.

"I'm in." Mak said with a smile.

"In? I wasn't. I'm not suggesting we . . . I just wanted to get this out there, to get someone's attention," Raj said.

"Well, you got it. Don't you dare send this to anyone else. Not another soul. Do you hear me? And, I want the email and physical addresses of anyone you did send it to."

"I . . ."

"Shhh." Mak put a finger to his lips with one hand and fumbled around in his suit jacket with the other, eventually producing an impossibly small notebook along with the world's tiniest pen. In it he wrote, "To Do: 1. Hire IP attorney. 2. Golf with Franky."

Franky was a relatively new friend Mak had met on the golf course a few months prior. They were supposed to be attending sessions at a conference, but had hit it off over dinner the night before and decided to get in18 holes instead. It turned out Franky was the founder of a private equity group, Greene Healthcare Holdings. Greene had amassed more than $100 billion in biotech and pharmaceutical assets. Franky would be just the place to start.

A round of golf, a few old-fashioned whiskey cocktails and two presentations later, Mak secured $10 million to get the ball rolling. To Greene, it was a bargain. With Raj and Mak, they had the brain, the brawn and a notable track record of success. And, if they delivered, it would be the biggest investment payoff in Greene's history. They quickly hammered out an agreement—Mak would own a third, Raj would own another, and Greene Healthcare Holdings the final third.

Mak and Raj hit the ground running. Raj immediately immersed himself in the project. Everything else in his life was pushed to the side—his family, his co-workers, even his appearance. Because he was no longer expected to fit into a larger corporate dynamic, he stopped shaving and grew a scraggly beard, he gained a bit of weight, and often wore a ratty T-shirt and jeans to work (thankfully obscured by his lab coat). Raj didn't care what he looked like. He felt liberated by being able to finally do direct battle with his nemesis, Alzheimer's.

Mak, for his part, did what *he* did best. He convinced every hotshot he had ever worked with, golfed with or walked past to join the effort. He knew and trusted almost every single one of the first 15. Most of them didn't know each other when they arrived, but they trusted and admired Mak. The whole place vibrated with engagement. It was awesome. Everyone felt as though they were working toward something not just important—but vital to humanity. It isn't every day you get asked to jump aboard a get-rich-quick, retire-early freight train whose first stop was safeguarding the sanity of the largest population of elders ever to walk the planet.

Sure, Mak could be a bit demanding and mercurial, sometimes sending people on wild goose chases that invariably ended in wasted time and effort. But that was just Mak. Everyone accepted his foibles because they believed in him. And, for a guy who lived by a ready, fire, aim leadership style, he sure did hit a lot of targets. Plus, as long as you executed Mak's plan, the rewards were abundant—even when it turned out to be a snipe hunt.

At first, everyone either reported to Mak or Raj. Eventually, a more formal structure emerged. To no surprise or objection, Mak became the chief executive officer (CEO) and Raj the chief scientific officer (CSO)—with a familiar cast of Mak's most loyal characters falling in around them in the standard C-suite roles (chief financial officer, chief human resources officer, chief quality officer, etcetera). It was a hard transition for those outside the top ring of influence since they had all signed on believing they were among Mak's closest and most trusted friends, but now found themselves one to three levels removed. Nevertheless, most of first 15 hung in there—which was more than anyone could say about the others. The 16th through the 75th (and beyond) seemed to be in constant churn.

Due to working long hours with laser-like focus, Raj made slow but methodical progress narrowing his three possible approaches to just two. Unfortunately, this pace wasn't fast enough to combat his mother's decline. About three years into their effort, Raj's mother passed. Regrettably, he hadn't been to see her in more than a month when he got the news. Raj coped by doubling down on his work.

Meanwhile, the private equity company recognized he was achieving solid results and gave the fledgling business more resources to strengthen its team. After six years, the company had swelled to roughly 110 people and was edging ever closer toward bringing Raj's revolutionary treatment to market. It seemed nothing could stop them.

While being without a product for several years is unusual for most businesses, pharmaceutical and biotech companies often went years before their first product hit the streets. It was the nature of the beast. At present, however, they were experiencing just a wee bit of a delay in preparing to start their clinical trials . . .

# CHAPTER ONE

# THE

# FOUNDER

Mak was a forward-thinking person. As soon as he awoke in the morning, he would mentally review everything he wanted to accomplish in the quarter and work backward to who needed to do what today to get it done. Then, he would write it all down in that small, weathered and so, so very "analog" notebook he kept with him at all times just in case he thought of an idea he didn't want to forget. Once he used up the pages, he'd grab a new one and start all over. He figured he had about a thousand of those tiny buggers in his desk drawers. Not that he ever looked back at them. *Tomorrow*, not yesterday or even today, was his motto. Like Wayne Gretzky said, ". . . skate to where the puck is going to be, not where it has been."

During the day, this notebook traveled with him everywhere, tucked away in his back pocket. The "kids" as he called them—in truth they were employees not that much younger than he—would tease him for not using his smartphone to tap out his thoughts. They would also joke about the funny face he made while writing in that microscopic thing. But Mak liked the physical feeling of penning reminders. He enjoyed being able to cross them off as he completed them. It gave him a feeling of accomplishment. And that face he made wasn't because he was struggling to see the words in front of him. It was actually the same face his farsighted father had made while writing. Perhaps, that is why the routine felt so familiar. So right.

This morning, however, he didn't feel like looking forward. Instead, as he shaved, he found himself reminiscing about the early days of the business he and Raj had started with Franky's help. They had come a long way since the first, small, rented space they used primarily to conduct interviews. Maybe it was time to acknowledge how far in a formal manner. Maybe they should hold a fancy dinner, no, a banquet. Yes, a *banquet*! They were definitely large enough to have a banquet. It would be an excellent way to reward the entire organization for its hard work.

He wrote in his notebook, in his rapid, almost-illegible scribble: *"Sked banquet to recognize progress and reward group. Show those who have something to be proud of that we are proud of them."*

This last line was a "Mak-ism," one of several proverbs he would think of during the day and memorialize in his notebook. One day, he thought, he might like to publish a small book of these chunks of wisdom. He often wondered how many he repeated since some had a familiar ring to them—but he never checked. *Ever forward.*

| | | | |

An hour later, Mak arrived at work. He parked his Tesla next to Raj's battered old Honda in front of the large building they leased. Then he double-checked his teeth in the mirror to make sure there was no spinach left over from the power shake he gulped down on the ride north from San Clemente.

Exiting his car, he headed for the entrance. Doing so, he observed the other colorless low-rises in this Aliso Viejo industrial park. There was a time when that sight had him nearly bursting with pride. Lately, however, all he could think about was how soul-sucking this drab commercial park was in spite of being located in Orange County, home of sunshine, beaches, and palm trees. They needed to get better digs—something better reflecting the impact they were about to have on the world. *Maybe he needed to do more than offer a banquet to his team. Perhaps he and Raj should move them into a more attractive site, maybe somewhere in Newport Beach or at least Costa Mesa? Surely, Franky would get it. Hell, it might even impact their valuation.*

Entering the executive suites, Mak saw Lauren bolt up from her chair in her office. She waved from the other side of the glass wall, mouthing something unintelligible but clearly indicating she wished to talk. Mak frowned. Lauren was a terrific chief financial officer (CFO), but she worried a little too much about the numbers. *If only we had a bit of revenue to distract her from blabbing about nothing but costs all day.* Mak smiled to himself as he rounded the corner to Lauren's office. He knew it was her job to bring him back to earth when he flew too high. But it was boring the hell out of him.

Mak's strategy with her, as with most people, followed the adage that a strong offense was better than a good defense. Entering her office, he shut the door behind him and spoke while she was in mid-sip of her morning coffee. "How long is our lease on this place? Wouldn't it be nice to be closer to water, or at least somewhere there's more to see and do?"

Lauren's lips, now free to respond, betrayed her purpose, pursing instead of parting. So, Mak continued. "I mean, don't you get tired of looking at all these squat concrete boxes?"

Lauren responded curtly, "Six months. There are six months left. But a move would be completely out of the question."

"Think about morale. We have to drive almost 20 minutes just to go somewhere with a view. We are in the middle of a concrete hell with heaven right next door!"

Lauren shook her head. "You're the only guy who would move an entire operation just to enjoy a poke bowl with a better view."

"Wrong. I hired most of these people over a poke bowl. It's not just me, it's everybody. We're cut off here. It's impossible to walk to anything from inside this industrial park. I mean, we're not Dunder Mifflin, are we? Don't we deserve better? We need a space we can enjoy, something cool and fun." He looked out at his busy office, reminding himself that none of this would exist if he and Raj hadn't made it happen. "I mean, look at what we've done here. No, actually, don't look, you'll gag; but I know you can feel it. We've built something special—only you'd never know it if you were driving by or sitting in one of our conference rooms."

Lauren shattered Mak's rhythm with one sentence. "We have to talk about the timeline."

He halted. "Yeah, I know, getting to Phase I is taking much longer than we thought, but we have to make sure there aren't—"

"Some of the people in the lab think Raj is going overboard on the details. He's changing up critical processes without informing clinical development and focusing on minutia that has no bearing on passing the next milestone."

Mak had to smile. "Whatever Raj thinks is important probably is. He's a certified genius, you know."

"Genius or not, right or wrong, it is irrelevant. The clock is ticking. At some point, we have to reverse the flow of cash. Franky wants a progress report at quarter's end. They have nearly doubled their initial investment already and Franky is signaling the well is drying up. I set up a pre-lunch meeting for us to discuss some reasonable measures—none of which contemplate spending more money, faster."

"A pre-lunch? Who says that? Let's *make* it a lunch . . . at the beach! I'll have Annie make a reservation at Kyoto. You know they have the freshest sashimi—"

"So, we're going to spend *more money* to talk about how we're spending too much money?"

Mak gave Lauren a beguiling smile, the one that always made her laugh in spite of herself. "Once in a while, we have to treat ourselves. We'll split dessert five ways, K?"

"Meaning you want me to invite the rest of the exec team?" But Mak had already turned and walked away.

| | | | |

Mak stopped at Annie's desk on the way to his office.

"Good morning, boss," Annie said in an upbeat tone. "Ready for the rundown?"

"Yes, please. No, wait, not just yet. Can you call Kyoto? See if we can book the back room for a lunch meeting around 12:30."

"Going for an outing, are we?" she said, picking up the phone.

"Indeed." Mak stood by her desk waiting for Annie to make the reservation and give him the rundown of what was coming off his schedule, working its way onto it, etcetera.

As Annie talked to the hostess, Mak saw Raj approaching. He shook his head at the ragged jeans and dirty sneakers under his partner's lab coat. The scene was so distracting to Mak, who always dressed to the tens (because the nines fell a little short in his mind). In his distraction, he almost missed Annie asking the hostess to push back an existing reservation under Lauren's name, versus making a new one . . . almost.

"And the winner for Techular Biologics Best-Dressed Man Award is . . ."

Raj ignored Mak's comment. He headed straight into Mak's office, indicating he should join him.

Mak looked back at Annie as he walked in and reached to shut the door, "Seems I've become a little too predictable. It sounds like Lauren only made lunch *seem* like my idea. I guess I'm gonna have to shake things up around here." He then mouthed the words, "I'm watching you two," while pointing to his eyes. Annie just smiled.

Before Mak turned around to face him, Raj blurted out, "Did you authorize this idiotic meeting Lauren set up? She gives us a few hours' notice for a meeting that will take me out of the lab for most of the day. What a colossal waste of time!"

"Um, yeah, she might have mentioned something about it. You heard about that already? It will be fun. We don't enjoy ourselves enough around here, especially you."

"Mak. C'mon, that's a long drive in the summer traffic and I've got *real* work to do! Besides, being dragged out of the lab to listen to Lauren drone on about cost projections isn't my idea of fun."

Mak flopped onto the bouncy ball he used instead of a chair. Raj sullenly watched as he bounced up and down writing in his notebook.

"Hey, I was thinking. I also want to hold a banquet for everybody," Mak said, trying to cheer him up. He never got around to springing it on Lauren so he tested it out on Raj instead. "We should celebrate what we've built, my friend."

"Celebratory dinners are best had after . . ."

"A banquet Raj, this will be a fabulous banquet, not some lousy dinner."

"Lunches, dinners, banquets. They are all just meaningless distractions. If you and Lauren want this done, you two—and the rest of the team—need to stop pulling me into endless meetings. I can't be bothered with this crap. And do you want to know what really pisses me off? *Money.* She wants to go faster for *money*, not for the lives I'm trying to save. Believe me, I am going as fast as I can—and not for a buck."

"Raj, pump the brakes. I understand. And I just told Lauren she has to trust you."

Raj blinked. "You did?" He paused. "Okay, perfect, so why do we need this idiotic meeting?"

"What do I always tell you?"

Raj sighed. "I don't know Mak, but I'm betting it's in that notebook. And more than once."

Mak smiled, "The squeaky wheel is just asking for oil." Then he looked back at Raj. "Sometimes you have to talk people through things. You can't always just insist on your way and not even explain the reasons for what you're doing. It's important to get people on your side—*to make the effort.*"

Raj refused to loosen his arms around his chest. "I hate wasting time."

"It's not wasting time if Lauren gets off your back for a few months, now is it?"

Raj didn't exactly smile, but the corners of his eyes crinkled. "Good enough."

| | | | |

The executive team sat at a long oak table with plates of tempura and specialty rolls before them in a private back room. An old-fashioned Japanese love song played on the speakers, complementing the simplistic black-and-white prints on the walls of seaside villages from a century ago.

Raj took a deep breath, "Lauren has a point. We should be honest with Franky. We need to let Greene know prepping for the trials is taking much longer than anticipated . . . and we will probably need a third round of funding to make it to market."

Everything stopped. Mak, who had just taken a bite of scallop, shook his head "no" as he chewed.

"Why not?" asked Lauren as Mak continued shaking his head.

Mak swallowed. "Franky's just the money man. Raj and I own two-thirds of the company. We don't tell Franky how to run Greene and Franky doesn't tell us how to run Techular. Exposing too much to Greene will open us up for more questions and more engagement. And trust me, you don't want that."

Lauren snapped back, "I don't think Franky likes being called that. I know I wouldn't. And we won't have a company to run if the money stops flowing."

"You're right Mak. They won't understand," said Raj. "It will just scare them into wanting more control."

"Maybe we should downsize? We ramped up in anticipation of

hitting the start date, but now we have several teams just standing by, waiting. Wouldn't that help the bottom line?" Larry offered.

"The problem, Larry, is all we have is a bottom line. A top line is what we need. We need revenue and pronto." Lauren exclaimed. Then she added, "But cutting head count would buy us some time."

Larry, the chief human resources officer (CHRO), was articulate but not quite as charismatic as Mak. Still, he had an eye for talent and was more organizationally savvy than the others . . . that went a long way in Mak's book, less so in Lauren's.

"We're not downsizing," Mak said sternly. "Shooting your own troops just shrinks the size of your own funeral." Mak repeated the line, this time to himself, as he scribbled it into his notebook. *Another good one.*

"I think we're going to need more time than anybody imagines," added Steve. Steve was the veteran of the group as its chief quality officer (CQO). "I'm actually concerned we're moving too fast. The lab has changed its protocols five times over the last several months and my team can't keep up with the constant shifting— even when we *are* notified."

"Whoa, shots fired, shots fired. Time out everyone," interrupted Mak. "Let's bring it down a notch."

"If you had some faith in my work, Steve," Raj began with an edge, clearly not taking it down a notch and causing their server to leave the plate she was in the middle of bussing. "You wouldn't worry. Mak and I built this company from nothing. Of course, we don't want anything bad to happen to it. Of course, we don't want to blow our timelines. Of course, I don't want to be changing my protocols."

"If we could just get an idea of how much time you need," said Lauren carefully, "Every time I try to pin you down on a date or a rough cost estimate . . ."

"Because it can't be pinned down! Because circling a date on a calendar or setting a number to it won't make it happen that way. I am working around the clock to figure out a way forward. And stupid gripe sessions like this don't help get it done any faster!"

Mak noticed Steve and Larry exchange concerned looks. He was glad they picked this spot in back of the restaurant away from the midday crowd. He didn't want word of their challenges to spread. Still, this exchange couldn't help but signal to everyone the conflict brewing between Raj and Lauren . . . and Steve and Raj . . . and Lauren and Larry. *That's about enough squeaking.*

This was the right moment to jump back in. "Okay. Okay. Lauren and Raj, we're all aware of your excellent people skills . . . please, stop showing off. The rest of us are starting to feel inadequate."

Mak knew only he could get away with teasing them into submission. Laughter exploded across the table. Even Raj chuckled.

"But seriously. Let's break this down. Raj. We know you are going as fast as you can. We know you are working night and day to solve problems no one else in the world has figured out. And Lauren, we also know we can't give tomorrow away for today. No one is dismissing your role or the value you add. These are exactly the right issues to be putting on the table at exactly the right time. We are all grateful to you for keeping us on our toes. Cash is the air this organization breathes. Without it, it will surely suffocate."

Somewhat assuaged, the little crease on Lauren's forehead softened. Mak threw Raj a pleading look. Raj had to know what that meant—time to do his part.

Raj turned to Lauren. "Yes. We are all appreciative for what you do."

Surprised, and perhaps not fully convinced, she stared back at him.

"You need to have an important voice here, I get that," Raj continued, a little uncomfortably. "I'm sorry. I will try to assemble a new timeline and have it to you in the morning. There are just complexities at hand that are difficult to account for, problems I could solve later today or not until next quarter," said Raj, trailing off a little bit at the end.

Mak surveyed the faces at the table, realizing the tension had dissipated. He smiled to himself. *Solace is always lurking in the shadows of anger.* He thought. *Another good one—I'm on fire today.* He quickly jotted it down as the team rambled on.

Less than an hour later, the group wobbled out of Kyoto, a little punchy from the food coma. As the afternoon traffic chugged up the Pacific Coast Highway and the sun shone down on them, Mak felt lighter than he did this morning. The view of Main Beach and the sound of the waves didn't hurt. *Too bad Laguna didn't have any commercial spots big enough for the labs.*

His team was back where they needed to be. Ever the bridge builder, Mak had successfully tended to the rift between Lauren and Raj, once again. It was only a matter of time before their treatment would proceed to the trials. And after that . . . well, the sky was the limit. Profits. Awards. Company growth. And more. Perhaps, there would be other indications (the pharmaceutical term for approved medical uses) for the plaque-dissolving biologic Raj was crafting. Maybe, just maybe, they could focus on something a little less depressing next time, like male-pattern baldness he thought, touching a portion of his head that used to contain hair.

Mak smiled to himself. He turned around to face the team as they walked down the street behind him, walking backward for a few steps so as not to slow the team's progress. "Today was good. Don't you think? Worth the price of lunch, eh Lauren?"

Lauren's response was drowned out by a painfully loud chorus of ear-splitting honks, one of which clearly belonged to something quite large. Mak felt the noise in the bottom of his gut. His legs locked and his back arched as an angry Prius passed so closely behind him that it almost twisted him around. He felt like a matador who had just escaped a raging bull. He locked eyes with his team—they were reaching for him, horrified. He cracked a small smile as his muscles relaxed and he regained control of his body.

The next thing to cross Mak's mind wasn't a thought. It was a large hunk of metal belonging to the side mirror of a tour bus whose horn was still trumpeting. Mak's body spun around and flopped forcibly to the ground. He landed on the hot pavement with his legs pinned behind him in an unnatural way.

"MAK!" Several people shouted at once.

The team crowded around him. Larry knelt down to check his vitals. Lauren waded into the middle of the street to prevent another strike. Mak's eyes were wide open and shifting from right to left. His breathing was shallow and unnaturally quick. Raj was down on all fours saying something he couldn't quite make out.

Mak's mind raced like never before. He panicked as memories of a family vacation danced across his psyche. Then, an idea struck, it was obvious. It was brilliant! *Wait, why hadn't it already occurred to Raj?* It was the answer they had been seeking. Raj had already figured out how to narrow down the field from three to two possibilities. Now, Mak had realized how to go from two to one.

*Forget about the pain. Forget about the blood. Clinical trials, here we come!* Despite everything, he had to write it down. But reaching for his notebook and pen, his body betrayed him.

*No . . .*

He tried to move again and again. All in vain. He looked up at Raj, frightened and unable to speak; his mind yielded to the darkness.

# CHAPTER TWO

# THE
# MONEY MAN

Franky was numb with disbelief. The CEO of one of Greene's most promising investments had been hit by a bus—right in front of his entire leadership team. It was every bit as grotesque as it was cliché.

*"What happens if you get hit by a bus?"* How many times had Franky used that exact line while explaining the need for succession planning with the CEOs in Greene's portfolio? How many times to Mak himself? Unbelievable!

It had only been a few days since the accident. Mak was on life support, and so, Franky feared, was Techular Biologics. Mak and Raj's unlikely partnership worked so well because each complemented the other. Raj was the brains. He loved to drill deep into the science (more often than not with brilliant results), while Mak's passion was running the place like the patriarch of a huge extended family. He had literally hand-selected more than half of the workforce and they stayed because they either believed he was going to change the world or make them rich . . . or both.

He ran the place like a benevolent puppet master—but they loved him for it. Everyone expected Mak to make the final decision on practically everything. And, rather than breed resentment and conflict, it prevented it. There was very little reason to duke out something with a peer. Instead, Mak would just listen to the argument and decide.

And that was that.

*But now the entire investment is at risk! There is absolutely nobody at Techular who can fill the void left by Mak. Nobody to tell the story—nobody to pull the strings. And, of course, nobody who wanted to address the leadership issue while Mak lay unconscious in a hospital bed, fighting for his life.*

Franky hated pressing business partners to focus on results. It felt so trite for a private equity firm—and it usually meant it was time to un-partner with them. This time, it was different. Franky needed a new CEO (and fast) but the circumstances and timing were just awful. Nevertheless, someone had to look out for the business . . .

Raj should get that. In fact, he should be all over it. But, of course, he won't be. Truthfully, Franky didn't know exactly what to expect from Raj. She had kept her distance over the years and dealt mainly with Mak and Lauren. Would he be an emotional mess, angry, or in denial? Either way, "ready to take command" wasn't a likely option from what she had seen . . . and heard.

Greene Healthcare Holdings had invested a big chunk of money—scratch that, *several* big chunks of money—and stood to take a major hit if this investment didn't pay off. Besides, not so different than everyone else, Franky was on this journey because of Mak. Surely Mak would not have wanted to see this dream fall apart at the seams. And surely, Raj didn't want to see that happen, either.

As Franky pulled into the parking lot of Techular, the stomach pains started. Franky knew the emotional cyclone that lay beyond those double glass doors. Undoubtedly, half the office would be in shock. The other half would be trying to talk it out. Few would be on task. It was a natural enough response. That it was happening wasn't the problem. The problem was no one was managing it. No one was leading.

Franky pulled down the visor and looked into the mirror.

She knew the woman staring back at her could handle this—whatever happened next. She had started out in quite the same way as Mak, as the founder/CEO of her own company. Only she discovered early on that being responsible for the people took a significant toll on her. She started Greene Healthcare Holdings with the fortune she made selling her first "baby." She was a natural businesswoman and a great leader, but she preferred seeding and advising businesses from behind the scenes to the pressure she felt standing at the helm.

The double-buzz of her phone pulled her out of her daze.

Gary: Good luck babe

Franky: Thumbs up emoji

She killed the engine and opened the car door. There was no sense delaying the inevitable. She gave her visage one more glance in the car window, pulling out the wrinkles in her suit jacket as she walked toward the front door.

| | | | |

As Franky strode through the open office area, exchanging muted greetings with the staff, she couldn't help sensing the anxiety in face after face. She gave them all a friendly, understanding I-feel-your-pain smile to provide a little comfort, a smile that only wavered when she approached the desk of Annie, Mak's assistant.

Franky could see the pain behind her swollen eyes.

"I—I just can't believe it," she said after a couple seconds of small talk. "It's was just so . . . random. It makes you question everything."

"Mak's not gone yet," Franky replied, although, deep down, she knew even the most optimistic of outcomes didn't put Mak back in his role. His condition was far too serious, and the doctors had given little encouragement about his chances.

"I know, Annie." Franky, mustering her most understanding

tone, one she hoped reflected confidence rather than uncertainty. "We all just have to hang in there. Ever forward, right?."

She nodded, managing a smile. "That's exactly what Mak would say. I'll go get Raj. He's in the lab. I think. We haven't really seen him around the executive offices much since . . ." her voice trailed off as she choked back a few more tears.

Franky patted her on the shoulder, "I'll wait in the conference room."

Franky sighed as she sat at the head of the empty table. It was worse than she had thought. Not only was Raj not leading when the team needed him most; he was hiding! Mak had been like a father, brother and/or a best friend to everyone here. He had emotionally "adopted" every person who ever worked for him as part of the secret sauce that made his managerial style so successful. It had made Techular an almost magical place to work.

*But what happens to the magic when the wizard is gone? What then?*

| | | | |

Through the conference room's glass wall, Franky noticed Raj making his way into his office (Raj never looked up once, as far as Franky could tell). Today's tattered look included wrinkled jeans that didn't quite fit, dirty Nikes, a stained lab coat and hair shooting every which way. Evidently Franky wasn't the only one nervous about this conversation. Raj telegraphed his anxiety by picking and chewing at his fingernails.

"Franky!" Raj jumped to his feet a little too quickly. Franky gave him a firm handshake, clasping the back of his right hand with her free hand in an effort to display her compassion for what Raj must be going through. "You okay?"

"Yes, yes, yes. Have a seat. What's on your mind? Oh, do you want a water or something? Coke? Diet Coke? Coffee?"

"No, thanks." Franky sat down in a cushioned chair. "How are things?"

"Well . . ." Raj remained standing.

"Raj, sit please. I know it's a hard time and I'm not here to make things more difficult."

Raj slowly sat and shook his head. "No, it's good, I'm glad you're here, Franky. Obviously, it's been hard since the accident, but you can see for yourself. We're still getting stuff done." Raj gestured toward the offices outside to indicate it was business as usual—which of course it wasn't—something Raj seemed to notice himself as he looked around for what seemed to be the first time in a while.

Franky nodded politely. "I stopped to see how he was doing on the way over. I don't mean to be blunt, but—"

"I know. I know. It's hard seeing him like that. I was there for a few hours last night." A pause. Raj's gaze drifted toward the back wall. "They say he may not come out of it. Ever. But I don't believe them." He turned back to Franky, almost defiantly. "Mak is a survivor. He's going to pull out of this, I know it. I've never known anyone stronger, more alive."

"Well, I'm pulling for him, too. You know how fond I am of Mak. But, even if he does recover, it's going to be a long road back. A very long road." Franky dragged out the second part of the sentence to drive home its meaning. "That's why I asked for this meeting." She took a breath. It was time for the hard part—for both of them. "We were already behind with the trials before the accident. We're undoubtedly going to be further behind as a result of it."

Raj was about to speak, but Franky held up a hand.

"That's not your fault—or anybody else's. It is just a fact. It's a natural consequence of an unforeseen tragedy. However, from this point on, we must do what we can to catch up. Leadership is going to be key in moving things forward."

"Oh, absolutely. I mean, luckily for us, Mak created a great organization here. Everyone knows their job, everyone knows what they have to do, so . . ."

*Are you kidding me! Did that bus hit you too?* Franky instantly felt guilty about her harsh feelings but couldn't believe her ears. Raj simply preferred the company of test tubes and Petri dishes to people. A feeling of real panic started to well up in her.

"I've had a few conversations with some team members," Franky continued carefully, trying not to show her feelings. "They're concerned that you're not—that really no one is, well, taking charge, communicating, pulling things together."

"Taking charge?" Raj said a bit too loudly. "Well, if anyone had bothered to come down to the lab, they would see I am doing what has to be done. The work of this company isn't done here in these offices. Who's telling you these things anyway? Everyone here knows what they have to do. I mean, I know Mak loved to be their personal cheerleader, but honestly, that kind of thing isn't necessary. This isn't a daycare center and I shouldn't have to hold anyone's hand. We're all grown-ups here. Anyone who doesn't know their role should pursue some other opportunity."

Franky nodded with a blank expression, not wanting to expose the depths of her concerns just yet.

"Is it Lauren?" Raj continued. "Don't bother, you don't have to tell me. I know she's the one who's complaining, because it's all about milestones and money with her."

Franky had to laugh. "Raj . . . what do you think it's about with me?"

Raj jerked his head back, as if waking from a dream. He realized he was indeed talking to the woman Mak had jokingly referred to as "the money man" for years.

"Franky, I'm sorry, we've all been on edge."

"Which is why I'm here, to make sure someone is attending to the people, the business and the science. I would never doubt you on the science, Raj. Never. But this team has been through a trauma, a horrible, unprecedented trauma. We have to keep this train on the tracks. But to be totally candid, you don't really have any leadership experience and yet all of this is falling on you, whether you recognize it or not. And it's just not your thing. Even you have to admit that."

"Admit that? Why would I admit that? I lead the lab staff and we get results every single day. Why wouldn't I be able to lead the rest of my company?"

"First, that is exactly what I want to hear you say. And not just say, but do. You have to actually do it, Raj. Otherwise, we need to get someone in here who can." Franky paused to put some space between the condescending way in which she had just said his name. She knew that kind of attitude wasn't going to get her anywhere.

Continuing in a more conciliatory tone, she said, "Not but 30 seconds ago you said you don't feel you or anyone else has to lead this company. You suggested it can lead itself. But it never works like that. Have you ever heard of the Hydra?"

Raj furrowed his brow. "The multiheaded monster?"

"Yes, that's it. It comes from Greek mythology. When it came after you, it didn't matter how many of those heads you cut off, more would immediately grow back. There was no way to stop it. My point is, that's what we're going to end up with here: a monster with a whole lot of heads that can't agree on anything. How will you make decisions, coordinate timelines, prioritize initiatives, provide oversight, etcetera?"

"Oversight? There is oversight. I am the oversight. And there will be no Hydra here. I can promise you."

"I appreciate that, and I'm certainly not saying you can't live up to your promise. I'm just asking you to maybe give this a little thought. Maybe your best and highest value to this organization is in the lab. Are you even ready to give up the labs? Who else could do it? Do you even want the responsibilities and demands that come with being a CEO? I can tell you from experience, it is a tough job. It isn't something you can just do on the side."

Raj said nothing so Franky plunged on. "You know you can't do both right? Especially since we're playing catch-up ball. Please tell me you know that." Franky cringed, knowing the desperation had crept back into her voice.

"Look. Mak and I were—are partners. This is *our* company," Raj responded with conviction.

"Excuse me?" Franky said sternly. "I think you're forgetting one critical partner, without whom you could not have done any of this."

"Yes, yes, it is yours as well. But you have taken a backseat since the beginning. Mak and I have been running this place together for six years. If Mak can't be here right now, then it's my job to run it. And I get it now. I hear what you are saying. I have to be the one to take care of *our* company."

*Ugh, he's entrenched now. He still thinks he can do it. He doesn't understand what it's going to take, and even if he did, he just doesn't have it in him. Time for plan B.*

|||||

It was almost too beautiful of a day for such a sad occasion.

Mak's wake was held in his home, overlooking the ocean. He was to be cremated the next day. Relatives, co-workers, and his daughter, Lily, who had recently graduated from Northwestern University, were scattered throughout the home. Franky watched Lily from afar, looking for the right moment.

She was impressed. Somehow, this 20-something young woman handled herself with grace and poise despite the circumstances. As Franky looked at her, she thought to herself, it was good she was so strong, because her mother hadn't been in the picture for years. She was now effectively an orphan . . . and a one-third owner of Techular, a fact Franky couldn't ignore.

Franky's stomach churned at the thought of what she was about to do. *It has to be dealt with, ASAP. It HAS to.* Franky repeated this mantra to herself as she prepared herself for action. Mixing work with wakes wasn't her idea of a good time, but she had no choice. She had to keep reminding herself she wasn't disrespecting Mak . . . or Raj for that matter. If anything, she was trying to save the company they had built from the ground up.

Franky's heart sank as she noticed a group of Techular staffers looking on while Raj slipped out the front door. *He had no idea what effect his actions had on other people. None.* Franky didn't need her mantra anymore. Raj had just given her all the motivation in the world.

| | | | |

"Lily, may I have a moment?"

Franky had been waiting in the corner of Mak's living room as Lily spoke with all the well-wishers, accepting their condolences graciously while trying to hold her own grief in check. This wouldn't be easy.

"Oh. Franky. Yes, just give me a second."

Franky stood by as a bespectacled aunt with thinning grey hair hugged Lily. She shot her husband a quick glance. Gary had posted himself across the room—he didn't want any part of this conversation. Gary nodded in Lily's direction, letting Franky know she was approaching. Franky guided her to the edge of the study so they could have some privacy without totally sequestering themselves.

"Lily, I am just so sorry. I didn't want to do this now. But I hope you realize I loved your dad and I believed in what he was doing. And I'm going to miss him very much. And, I am just so sorry for your loss."

Lily nodded, looking as if she was waiting for the other shoe to drop.

"But, as I said on the phone, I'm concerned about the business. We really need to create a leadership succession plan as quickly as possible. Things are not going well. Your dad is irreplaceable, but there are plenty of talented executives who we could—"

"Franky, I don't mean to be disrespectful, but I just lost my father. I really don't want to get into this right now."

"Lily, anyone in your position would say those same words. But anyone in my position would tell you we don't have the luxury of waiting. Everything your father built is at risk. There's a leadership vacuum at the office and, if it isn't addressed, we could lose everything—you, me, Raj, the employees, everyone."

Lily took a deep breath. "My father would have wanted Uncle Raj to take over. He never got the chance to actually say that, but it's the truth. Raj probably needs a little time to recover from this too, then I'm sure he'll—"

Franky couldn't stop herself from interrupting. "Raj? Where is Raj, Lily? Is he helping lead you through this trying time? What about the scores of employees scattered about this house? Is he leading them?"

Lily looked around with mild confusion. "He must be somewhere. I just saw his son a minute ago."

"He ducked out 20 minutes ago. I'd bet the farm he's back in the lab. Now that's a dedicated scientist. But it is in no way, shape, or form a dedicated leader. Raj needed to stay here and be with you. He needed to be with the rest of the team during this crucial time. He needed to help them heal."

To accentuate his point, Franky glanced over at Lauren, Steve, and a few other Techular employees gathered in their own little group, looking lost and sad. Lily followed her gaze and saw for herself what Franky was talking about. She looked down at the floorboards, as if she were beginning to understand.

"I know what you're saying. But I also know what you want. You want me to vote Raj out, but I . . ." Her voice broke just a little. "I think Dad would have hated that. It's something he never would have done if he were still . . ."

She wiped fresh tears from her eyes. Franky felt for her. She wanted to hug her, to tell her things would be okay. But she needed Lily to tap into her strength, not collapse into herself. "It's not about what he would have done, Lily. It's about what needs to be done. Your father trusted me. I think you know that."

"Yes, he did."

"And for the most part, I've been a silent partner. *Very silent.* Just 'the money man,' as he used to joke." They shared an uncomfortable smirk—evidently Lily knew about the moniker and was about as comfortable with it as Franky. "Now, I have to speak up. And you need to find your voice, too. It isn't just about the money, although there's plenty of that at stake for us both. Think about all those people. She glanced over in the direction of the executive team again. We need to make sure this company doesn't fail."

"But Uncle Raj . . ." She looked around as if she expected him to pop up.

"He will remain a vital part of Techular. I will assure you of that in writing."

Lily nodded, seemingly put at ease by the notion that Raj wouldn't be kicked out of his own company.

"You just earned a degree in journalism, if I remember," Franky continued. "Well, then you're trained to gather and appreciate facts. Ask around. Interview a few members of the leadership team. You'll quickly find I am not alone in my beliefs. Furthermore, Raj may not even know it consciously, but I bet he'd actually be happier with a real leader back at the helm. He can barely lead his lab, let alone the entire company."

Lily stood perfectly still for a few moments as she deliberated. Once again Franky found herself admiring Lily's poise. For such a young person, she seemed to have it surprisingly together. Franky tried to appear as calm as possible, but her insides were in knots. There were a hundred or so people and a few billion dollars riding on Lily's next words.

"Give me a couple of days to think," Lily finally said. "I'll also talk to some members of the team. Then, we can chat. But I'm not promising anything."

"Good enough."

*More than good enough. Exactly the words I wanted to hear.*

| | | | |

Franky put away her phone. Raj was burrowed so deep into his work that she couldn't even get him to return a text most days—let alone meet with anyone. *Why is he still blocking the idea of a professional CEO? It's not like he's doing the job!*

The clock was ticking and Franky was running out of options. Raj's leadership skills had certainly not improved since their original talk and the situation at Techular was getting worse by the day. It had been two months since Franky had intervened with Lily at the service and about five months since the accident. Unfortunately, Lily insisted on getting Raj on board with any changes and she wouldn't even consider selling her stake.

*She is as loyal as she is strong. I hope there is something left of her inheritance when we liquidate. Oh, I hope it doesn't come to that. Please let this plan work! What is this, plan C . . . D?*

At the moment, Franky sat on the sofa in her office beside her second-in-command Bob Griffiths. They were trying to choose who would be the best CEO candidate to "forcibly" introduce to Raj. They already had eliminated more than 15 candidates. Now it was down to three, all of whom were gifted, proven executives. In the personal interviews, however, one outshone all others in Franky's mind. As a matter of fact, she didn't even feel it was a contest.

"So—what do you think?" she asked Bob, as they stared down at the three resumes on the coffee table between them.

"Well, I know what *you* think," Bob said teasingly. "You want Andy. And I agree, he's a superstar. But it's hard to imagine a guy like that mixing it up with Raj on a daily basis. And he doesn't have a technical background. They will be like oil and water."

"Andy will run the business and Raj will run the science. It will be like when Mak was running the show. Andy's by far one of the best executives I've ever seen. He's got the exact right instincts to get people on his side and keep them motivated. He doesn't even have to think about how to do it, he just *knows*. Besides, he's had extensive experience in the sector. Raj can't pick at his credentials. They are impeccable."

Bob laughed, "I think we both know Raj is not operating within the boundaries of logic here. But, like I said, I know what you think about Andy. I think your mind is made up."

"Then let's get them together."

"So, just how are you going to do that again? Raj hasn't answered a single one of your calls and only sometimes answers your texts."

Franky allowed herself the smallest of sighs. No use showing Bob the true fear ruling her stomach these days, forcing her to chug Pepto Bismol between meetings. "He's in denial and he's going to be a problem. But those are the cards we've been dealt no matter who we pick. We need to do something. I'm going to try him again in a few minutes and see if I can get him to agree to a breakfast or lunch. If that doesn't work, it'll have to be an ambush date."

Bob smiled a sideways smile back at her, not hiding his skepticism one bit.

"Don't worry, I got this." Franky said confidently, wishing she felt as good about this decision as she let on. The truth was everything rode on Andy now. Somehow, they would have to convince Raj that this was the right way to go. Steeling herself, Franky picked up the phone to make the call. This was it.

*Come on Raj, pick up buddy, pick up.*

# CHAPTER THREE

# THE

# EXPERT

Raj could not believe his ears. His entire team was huddled around the conference room table complaining about him . . . and right to his face! He had literally just paved the way to saving their jobs—and eradicating this wretched disease. But, instead of showing any sense of gratitude or excitement, they were coming at him guns blazing.

The breakthrough Raj was hoping to celebrate had come after months of relentless work. Finally, he had determined which of his original three paths was the route to success. They were now ready to pull the trigger on Phase I of their clinical trials. Meanwhile, he was at the point where he didn't even know what day it was—time had lost all meaning to him. The only thing he held onto was not letting Mak's memory down. A part of him knew the pace of his work in the lab had distracted him from dealing with the loss of his partner and best friend—still, the results spoke for themselves. Soon, they would be able to go full blast at the trials. But, instead of celebrating, his team was acting like a bunch of children, bickering like fools.

If they only knew the whole story, he thought. He didn't want to create too much of a stir by sharing just how precarious the situation had been, particularly since none of them could do anything to help. For months he had been terrified he had hit an unbreakable roadblock. It had been entirely possible that none of his approaches would work. Nobody really knew about the 24/7 stress he had been living with since discovering a flaw in his original logic.

Now, *finally*, he could relax a bit and spend some time tending to the rest of the organization (like he had promised Franky). Or so he had thought.

To celebrate his achievement, he decided to have a working lunch with the executive team—it had been quite a while since their last staff meeting. He was afraid to have it offsite given the trauma of the last lunch outing. To circumvent Lauren's spending complaints (which had only gotten louder and more frequent due to the continued delays), he paid for pizza out of his own pocket, along with soft drinks, bottled water, and juices—not just for the people in the meeting, but everyone at the company. He wanted to show them all he knew how tough the last several months had been.

Sure, he knew he had isolated himself from the rest of the business, but, getting this treatment ready *was* the business. Someone needed to keep this company afloat. And, he had done it. He had finally removed the last obstacle to starting the trials. It was the giant step forward they needed and he wanted everyone to share in the excitement.

So . . . free pizza, free soft drinks, and an open forum to celebrate successes and plan forward. Sadly, complaints were all anyone offered. Watching the calamity, he had the vague sense that it might not have been the best idea to expect them to join in celebrating his defeat of a crisis they never knew existed.

Everyone in the conference room seemed to be angry—and not in general—specifically at him!

Raj refocused on the team's conversation in time to process the end of Larry's rant. "I mean, didn't you even think to say something to someone? You just told this guy he was *hired* and had him show up for his first day! Without letting anyone else even know? *I'm* supposed to vet and process all new personnel. Did you even get a resume? Did you check his references? Employment history? Did he take a drug test? Did you put him in the system? How exactly did you think he was going to get paid, get health insurance?"

*Ugh.* Larry. Everyone seemed to love this guy. To Raj, he was just another bureaucrat who demanded appeasement at all costs.

"I already explained all this," Raj knew his words were coming out impatient and annoyed, but he couldn't help it. Besides, at this point, he didn't care. He was the head of this company, despite Franky's continued pestering. He didn't need Larry's permission. "I sent Dr. Warren to you to get those things done. I didn't need a resume. The world has been adequately informed of Dr. Warren's accomplishments through his work. Frankly, he is the only qualified candidate in this hemisphere. I needed his expertise, so I could get out of the lab enough times a week to run the company. I've known Dr. Warren for 15 years. The entire scientific community knows him. Five minutes on the web and you could have answered all those questions yourself—are you here to help or hinder our progress, Larry?"

Before Larry could answer, Lauren jumped in. "Well, I hope he's gonna replace you—he's sure getting paid like it."

What a surprise, Lauren complaining about spending. Soooo unexpected.

"You guys are missing the big picture, all right? We just cleared a huge hurdle that threatened to end this entire enterprise and, when we finally did it, I must say I didn't see any of you to my right or left . . . but I did see Dr. Warren."

*So ungrateful. I am the hero here—not the villain!*

Raj was so angry he didn't even want to look at the team anymore. To prevent seeing any more eye-rolling, he went to refill his cup though it was still half-full.

"Raj," said Steve, using his annoying *"Hey, I'm your bud"* tone he put on—he liked to act as if he were the only grown-up in the room—"everyone's just a tad frustrated. People are running in a hundred different directions. We all know you've been buried in your work, but . . . well, this company is more than just the labs—and you're supposedly running the whole thing. Sure, the rest of it exists to support the labs; but we can't do that if you don't let us. And, this is the first we're hearing of some crisis other than the missed milestones and exodus of the lab staff."

"Well, I'm not Mak. Don't expect me to run things like him. Mak is gone! I was doing my best to save what we built together—to save your jobs!"

Raj awkwardly turned his back to the group again, wincing at his own harshness as he poured more Coke. It foamed over the top of the cup. Hands shaking, Raj grabbed a napkin to wipe up his mess. He was instantly sorry for what he said. Then, suddenly he wasn't. He knew everyone missed Mak. *He* missed Mak. Mak was his best friend. But nobody seemed to care about *his* feelings. He turned just in time to see Lauren and Larry exchange more eye rolls.

*These are the people I work all hours for. The ones who laugh at me when I'm not looking. Totally awesome.*

"None of you gets it," Raj muttered as he sat back down.

"Do *you* get it, Raj?" Larry asked, challenging him. "How well our company runs is a big part of how the outside world sees us. If we seem disorganized—at loose ends, who's going to trust anything that comes out of this place? What do you think all these people are saying about us after they walk out that door? Do you know how hard it's getting for people to trust we're ever going to get this treatment to market?"

"We don't need trust. We have science. The clinical trials will provide the facts. And thanks to hard work, not whining, those trials are not going to be a problem. We've made a significant breakthrough, Larry. Very significant. And you're all acting like it's nothing."

"This so-called breakthrough—which you've told us nothing about—just puts us back where we were supposed to be months ago. We're almost at twice the burn rate we projected in our operating budget," Lauren responded. "That's also significant. Especially when I'm the one who has to deal with the blowback. When Franky looks over this quarter's balance sheet, especially this new hire's excessive salary—"

"Fair market price!" Raj barked. "I got Dr. Warren at fair market price. And it was my decision to make!"

"This is the kind of thing Mak kept Franky in the loop about, because it's a big expense. We are running out of cash, Raj, and I don't think Greene's is going to just slap down the extra cash without making some changes around here."

"Excuse me. Just what are you implying, Lauren?" Raj raged again. He was very uncomfortable with Lauren's relationship with Franky. Lauren always talked as if she worked for Franky, not Mak and Raj.

"Let's all calm down." More from soothing Steve. "Raj, we realize how hard you've been working. Maybe a little too hard . . ."

"There may very well be some changes around here," muttered Raj. He was still fuming about what Lauren said, regarding changes. He wondered if she knew Franky had been trying hard to push for him to step down.

Just then, Annie poked her head inside the room. "Raj, Franky's here to see you. She said it's urgent."

"What?"

"Better see what she wants. Sounds important." Lauren said in a tone so condescending it nearly burst the blood vessels in Raj's neck.

Raj looked around him. This meeting was beginning to feel more like an orchestrated mutiny than a run-of-the-mill gripe session. He turned to Lauren, who stared daggers back at him. She clearly knew something. The looks on the faces around the room also suggested they knew something was up. Raj realized he had no friends in this conference room. *They've been ratting me out. Running behind my back to tell Franky a bunch of crap. The ingrates. There wouldn't even BE a company without me. When was the last time I saw a single one of them in the lab? Other than Steve, I can't remember a single time—let alone the last time!*

Annie was still standing with her head halfway in the room. He could tell she was incredibly uncomfortable.

"Have her wait in my office. I will be there in a bit."

Annie nodded and shut the door behind her.

"Meeting over." Raj said angrily.

| | | | |

Raj sat in the empty meeting room for a few minutes after the team left. He had a bad feeling about Franky's unannounced visit. Perhaps he had blown her off one time too many. *But why hadn't Lauren told him the cash problem had gotten so bad? Wasn't that her job? Well, whatever, Franky can't do anything to me anyway. She can't fire me and she can't pull the funding. Greene would lose the millions they already spent and the billions they know they're going to make. She needs me as much as I need her.*

Raj stood up. He was feeling a little more in control, but his legs were shaky from the adrenaline dump. He tried to calm down by taking deep breaths as he walked across the hall to his office.

But it didn't help that Franky dispensed with all pleasantries and cut to the chase the second he sat down. "I need you to come to dinner with me tonight," she said, seated in the chair beside his desk.

"Are you kidding me? You interrupted my staff meeting to invite me to dinner?"

Franky shrugged, "Well, you wouldn't answer my calls or texts and I know what your inbox looks like. Our reservations are for 6 p.m."

"Six? It's only three o'clock!"

"I know but I thought you might need some warning. And time to collect yourself." Franky said motioning in Raj's general direction.

"Are you suggesting there's something wrong with how I look?"

"No. I, I just thought you might want to get some things done and freshen up before dinner."

"Wait . . . are you saying I am unkept? Are you embarrassed to be with me?" Raj could tell his pushback had taken Franky by surprise.

Of course, Raj knew his nutty professor look wouldn't fly for dinner, but he liked pushing Franky onto the ropes a bit, particularly after the day he'd had.

"No, no, no, Raj, I was trying to respect the fact that you work long hours *and* you weren't planning on this dinner *and* you might appreciate some time to clean up a bit, change your clothes, whatever."

"You're out of line." Raj could see Franky was getting uncharacteristically flustered. He had thrown her off balance and he liked it. Deep creases mottled his forehead. He stared at Franky and let it get just a bit more uncomfortable. "Okay, whatever," he said, deciding it wasn't worth pushing any further. "I mean . . . I guess you have a point. I've already been at it for 10 hours today." As he said those words, some real exhaustion set in. In the past 90 minutes he had gone from zero to 60 back to zero a dozen times.

"I believe it. You look rundown. Truthfully, I'm worried about you. So is everyone else, but no one seems to be able to get through. Something has to change or we're going to be in more trouble than we already are."

"*Trouble?* What trouble?"

"Well, what if something were to happen to you? We'll talk at dinner. The reservation's at Candicci's. Do you want to drive together or meet me there?"

"Um. I'll drive myself. I'll leave here in a few and go home to change."

"Good. I am looking forward to it. There's someone I want you to meet. I'm hoping you two will hit it off."

Alarm bells went off in Raj's head. "Someone you want me to meet? Who are you springing on me? What is this?"

Franky was already getting up. "Nothing to worry about. We'll talk at dinner."

As Franky exited Raj's office, he sat back in his chair, angry with . . . everyone. He looked around his disheveled office. Maybe he *had* let things go too far. Maybe his tunnel vision *had* become too extreme. Maybe he needed Franky's wake-up call. He made a mental note to apologize at dinner. Franky was an ally—a partner really. She had been there since the beginning. Mak always trusted her. But then again, she always stayed out of his hair.

*It's fine. I'll apologize at dinner.*

But then Raj remembered Franky said she was bringing someone to dinner. *What is she up to?*

| | | | |

"Raj, meet Andy Newsome. Andy, this is Raj."

Raj did his best to smile. But inside, he seethed. He didn't want to make a scene but it had occurred to him on the way over that this was probably an interview. Andy looked at the other two, trying to judge if he should sit first or wait for Raj and Franky to sit. Raj ignored Andy's dilemma and plopped down first. Franky smirked at Raj and signaled for Andy to take a seat.

Andy spoke first, "I've heard amazing things about you, Raj. I hear your Alzheimer's treatment is going to be an incredible breakthrough!"

*Nice try. Flattery will get you nowhere with me, pal.*

Raj nodded his head and gave a slight smile. Meanwhile, Franky ordered a bottle of wine. An expensive one. She was sure laying things on thick.

"So, who is Andy and what are we doing here?" Raj asked Franky.

Franky's plastered-on smile never wavered. "I think you know exactly what this is about. Andy is the CEO candidate I've been trying to get you to discuss."

"I already gave you my answer. Sorry to waste your time, Andy." Raj snapped.

"I can see you're just not getting it. It's like this. You either accept Andy's partnership or I'm pulling our support, Raj. End of story." Raj opened his mouth to say something, but Franky held up her hand, cutting him off. "Andy has got a ton of experience. We'd be lucky to have him."

Raj began to launch into a response when suddenly, *infuriatingly*, the server showed up again with the expensive bottle of chardonnay.

"And what are we celebrating tonight?" she asked, uncorking it.

Raj grit his teeth. Andy lowered his eyes. Only Franky ventured a response. "To our continued success."

"Lovely." The server poured a little in Franky's glass.

She took a taste and nodded. Raj was about to explode.

"Honestly," Andy said to Raj in an attempt at pacification. "I can only begin to imagine how hard this must be to even consider . . ."

Raj tried to smile but was sure it looked more like a grimace. He fumed inside as the server finished filling their glasses *as slowly as humanly possible*. When she placed the bottle in a nearby ice bucket at last, Raj ventured to say something more but Franky cut him off.

"We'll need a few more minutes before we order," she said to the server. Again smiling. *What a pro.* It irritated him to see how good she was at this. Still, the second the server scooted off to her next table, Raj leapt to his feet as if his chair had suddenly been electrified.

"Franky, I'd like a word."

"Raj, please."

"Outside. In private."

"There's no need for that," Franky responded calmly, as if he expected this kind of reaction. "Please. Sit down. There are no secrets here. Andy signed a non-disclosure agreement. We can talk the whole thing through together—even the unpleasant parts."

Raj said nothing. He headed toward the exit without looking back. Once outside, he breathed in the cool night air, realizing he'd been holding his breath since standing. He looked off toward the silhouette of the rolling hills in the distance. And waited.

"Raj."

"You think you get to do this to me? Do you know what I've been through to get us where we are? Look at me Franky. Look at me."

"I am Raj. I see what it's doing to you. That's kind of the point."

"No, it's not. It's not the point at all. Where have you been? Why do you think you get to lob all these bombs in my direction? Why does all this fall on me?"

"Raj, I am trying to get you the help you need."

"All of your talk about the people, what about the team? Who is going to pull it all together? Empty talk. You haven't been willing to lift one finger to fix a thing. Meanwhile, I've been killing myself, working around the clock to make sure all of those people you pretend to worry about have jobs—that we have a product!"

Franky reached out to put her hand on Raj's shoulder but he moved away.

"Don't patronize me!"

"Raj, I'm aware there was some kind of breakthrough in the lab; I was getting a download from Lauren on the way over. That's wonderful. Truly, it's wonderful. I'd love to hear more. It sounds like we're ready for the trials. Let's go back inside and discuss it. It's coming at just the right moment. I don't think we could have sustained any more delays. But, the truth is you've got the rest of your team ready to throw in the towel. They are running around in circles fighting each other because you're not giving them the time of day, let alone any direction. The only thing they can agree on is their frustration with you. And, who knows, you might have achieved that breakthrough sooner if you had let them help. Steve could have helped . . . and speaking of clinical development—you might be ready for the trials, but they aren't. If we're going to get this drug to market, we have to clear the way for it. And that's not just a matter of getting the science right. It's about the whole picture: funding, patient safety, compliance, and, people, most of all people. You can't ignore the people, Raj."

"Look, I don't know what Lauren told you, or the others for that matter. Obviously, you're talking to all of my people, but this was serious. I didn't tell them or you because I didn't want to create panic. We had only two paths left and it didn't look as if either of them were going to work. It took everything I had and every moment I had to figure our way out of this mess. All of this, all of it, would have been for nothing, Franky. The company, Mak's death, none of it. I either solved this problem or we all went home! It is as simple as that.

Franky started to say something, but Raj cut her off.

"I refuse to be the villain of this story. I'm the one who saved the day." Raj was really feeling on a roll now. Franky was on her heels, so he kept pressing, "And then you—you interrupt my celebration with this, this betrayal? Where were you when I needed you? Where was anybody? You have no right to do this. I own a full third of this company and none of this will go anywhere without me!"

"Raj, I've tried to reach you. You have been alone because you chose to be. You left me no choice. Please, just give Andy a chance. Please. There is so much at stake for all of us."

Raj turned to go. Before he left he wheeled around to face her. "What are you talking about? You've been to my office twice since Mak died. What have you done except plot behind my back? You want to know the difference between us? When I see something that has to be done, I do it. If you want to help, get in the game. Otherwise, get out of my way!"

# CHAPTER FOUR

# THE

# CEO

It was worse than she had imagined. Franky knew before stepping back through the doors at Techular that the team was in a downward spiral. After all, it's what forced her hand. *But for things to fall apart this much, this fast?* It was a new level of crazy.

The problem with Raj's criticisms at dinner a few weeks ago is that they were all too true. She had spent the last 15 years removing herself more and more from the daily grind, lobbing money and advice (and sometimes talented people) over the fence to help her companies succeed. But then again, it felt as if whenever she stepped back, (thankfully), other people stepped up. And they made millions together.

It's not that Franky didn't know how to dig in. Quite the opposite. She had a unique gift for showing empathy and respect for others while driving relentlessly for results. And, having been a part of so many successful transactions and turnarounds, she had learned even more since her days in the trenches. The problem for Franky wasn't ability or even energy. No, her problem was that the closer she got to the action, the more responsibility she felt for, well, everything.

Pushing these feelings aside, she had expected her arrival to bring with it some initial relief. She also expected some sense of decorum with a touch of hidden backstabbing here and there—as well as a heaping scoop of passive (and not-so-passive) aggressiveness from Raj.

She was, no surprise, correct about Raj, but startlingly wrong about the others. Nothing in her years of experience had prepared her for the shout fest that erupted just as soon as she arrived. *Maybe my husband was right. . . . Maybe I should have steered clear of this one.*

"What do you need this for?" Gary had said after she told him her plan. "This place sounds like a circus. Are you sure they will ever have an actual product? And Raj is a train wreck! Just let it die on the vine. Every bet doesn't come up a winner. Can't you just move on and make it up on the next one?"

She knew what was coming next. He would sing the song. She hated it when he sang the song. And yet, at the same time, she kind of loved it. Gary was a bit of a kook. The yang to her yin, he always lightened things up at her darkest moments.

*"Oh, Franky . . . you give and you give without taking . . . you don't need it today . . . oh, Franky . . ."*

It was Gary's version of Barry Manilow's "Mandy," with his custom—and out-of-tune—lyrics. He loved to serenade her whenever he felt she was pushing herself too hard, which was, well, often. She couldn't help it. Her responsibilities always weighed so heavily on her. Gary was a nice balancing force, but she rarely backed off, no matter how many verses he sang. The two of them were just built differently. Gary was an attorney, but not a "biller," his term for those diehard partners who still logged insane hours as if they were junior associates. Gary worked until the day was done, then shut it all down until the next day.

When he was finished belting his song, Franky said what she always said: "You're no Manilow."

To which Gary gave his standard response, "I don't have his echo chamber at my disposal."

"Look, it's been a while since I've gotten this involved but it will be okay. I'm not so bad it."

"That's an understatement. You're amazing and everybody knows it. But do you really want the headache? Don't forget, I was there for your first rodeo. And every single one since. It's been so much better on you since you assumed the investor role. Can't you let somebody else do this?"

"You know the answer to that. Raj won't let anyone else past the front door and Lily wouldn't sign off on anybody but me as CEO."

"I know, babe. And I don't want to make it any harder on you. I know you'll succeed. I'm just worried about the toll it'll take."

"I'll turn things around and get out. Two years. Tops."

"*Two years?* Ugh, I was kind of hoping for sooner. But you're right. These things don't turn on a dime. Then again . . ."

Oh, hell, he was going to sing again.

"*Oh Franky . . . will you quit this and stop me from singing . . .*"

She laughed. "Okay. That's enough. I don't want to hear your version of 'Copacabana.'"

Of course, she knew by saying that, she would have to.

"*His name was Gary . . . he married Franky . . .*"

But all that was weeks ago, just after the fires from the argument with Raj had forged her resolve. Now, playtime was over. And she was wincing from the overwhelming headache rapidly mushrooming inside her skull. She had only slept two hours the night before, if that, and it was catching up with her.

Still, the facts hadn't changed and unfortunately, she was the only one who could slip in and help untangle this mess. She knew she couldn't count on Raj for much. Her only hope had been the rest of the executive team would welcome her presence enough to engage and work with her toward solid solutions—a hope that was quickly evaporating.

Franky quickly discovered the senior staff didn't care what she had to say. It's like she actually held more sway from the outside, when she was the 'money man.' This team only cared about what *they* had to say. Their level of frustration was sky-high, because Raj, the final authority on everything until the moment she crowned herself CEO, hadn't been responding to any of their concerns. He was a like a horse running down the track with blinders on. Meanwhile, the world was falling apart. Pivotal vendors were threatening to stop working with Techular—for the astoundingly dumb reason that Raj hadn't processed a single invoice in months. No surprise, Lauren was furious, seemingly too furious to fix a problem she should have been able to spot.

Larry revealed numerous complaints had been filed by lab employees due to Raj's explosive temperament. And Steve reiterated his lack of readiness for the trials due to last-minute changes that hadn't been properly communicated to his team. Delays and disorganization *now* were better than delays and disorganization encountered once the Food and Drug Administration (FDA) was involved, Steve insisted. And, he was right. Of course, Raj's name came up at the center of almost every dispute; but the real problem was Franky couldn't find any binding agent between the executives other than their mutual disdain. This team only knew how to coordinate attacks . . . not work.

Franky had seen enough. As politely as possible, she stopped Steve midsentence by saying, "We are not going to even try to meet the current schedule." After all, she reasoned, it was an arbitrary date to begin with. *Why compound our internal problems just to hit it?*

"Don't worry. I am releasing the additional capital," Franky added.

"You can't do that!"

Those were the first words Raj had spoken all day. Every department head turned to face their disheveled (and disgruntled) chief scientific officer at the other end of conference table.

"And why not?" Franky asked, careful to not let an edge creep into her voice. She was hoping to use this meeting to actually pull Raj in her direction.

"Why? Why? Because we're finally ready to go. I rode myself and my team to the brink of exhaustion for months to make it. We worked night and day to get us to where we are and I'm not going to watch you throw all that hard work away so you can flex your muscles before you even have the slightest sense of what the consequences will be."

"It's her call," Steve responded angrily. "And it's about time someone made a decision!" Steve looked like he was about to launch into more invectives when Franky stopped him. *Throwing another bucket of negativity into Raj's face wouldn't get them anywhere.*

"Let me stop you there," she said, sucking the air out of his tirade. Steve stood frozen in time for a moment as if the director had just yelled "cut" in the middle of a poorly chosen improvisation. "Let's all remember that we're here to realize a vision born the day Raj's mother was diagnosed with a death sentence, one that affects 10 percent of adults over the age of 65. Furthermore, in the wake of your boss's—but his best friend's—death, Raj locked himself in our lab with one thought: keeping this vision and this company alive. His work has just saved your jobs. He is, and will continue to be, one of our largest shareholders and a vital member of this team. If you aren't willing to work with him or any of your other colleagues because of the calamity that has befallen this company in the wake of Mak's death, I invite you to leave."

She paused to let this "invitation" settle in the room. She assumed there would be no takers but wasn't bluffing. She took a deep breath and softened her tone.

"None of you deserved what happened. From what I can see, it has taken a toll on each and every one of you. You do not have to forgive each other. You do not have to forget. And you do not have to stay. But staying does imply a commitment to putting this team back together, healing this organization, and getting this treatment to market. Statements and actions contrary to those purposes will be considered notice of your resignation. We are at an inflection point, after which we . . ." she paused and repeated herself for emphasis, ". . . *we* cannot tolerate movement in the wrong direction. The state of things is too precarious."

Raj shifted in his seat. Franky could tell her words (which she had planned the night before) had hit their mark. Raj wanted to fire off a reply to Steve's nasty remark and continue the debate regarding her timeline suggestion. However, he couldn't muster the right response. Franky had hoped to see a glimmer of pride shine through; instead she saw a wave of sadness spill over his anger as her words sunk in.

"Now, as for the timeline," she said, returning to Raj, "The problem is clinical development has to catch up with what you've accomplished. If the documentation isn't letter-perfect and our actions, and those of our vendors, don't follow it to the letter, the FDA will stop us in our tracks, setting us up for more delays and more scrutiny. I've seen that movie before and I'm not signing up to produce the sequel."

Silence from the room. Filling the vacuum, Franky plodded on.

"I just want everyone to know," she said, since she hadn't really gotten the chance to talk about her leadership philosophy, "this isn't about a power trip. I don't do power trips. I don't even know how to pack for one."

*A little laugh from half the room. That's something.*

"Here's my process. We need to hear everyone's viewpoints, particularly when they are divergent, so we can consider all the facts, perceived opportunities and risks. When we can't reach a decision together, or when I vehemently disagree, I will make the call on whether we need more time to align or I need to go it alone. But each time I make a decision by myself, I'll do it knowing it weakens us as a team."

"Well, that's different from Mak," Lauren smiled, adding, "May he rest in peace." A few members of the team joined in a quiet chuckle. "He'd just talk us into thinking we wanted to do what *he* wanted us to do."

"That was his specialty," Larry added, laughing. Then his tone changed. "But I have to be honest—Mak would have moved heaven and earth to make this deadline. Maybe we should consider an attempt."

"Let's do it," Lauren nodded. "That's what Mak would have wanted."

*But Mak isn't here and you people will kill each other if I don't relieve some pressure, pronto! We are hurtling toward disaster.*

Franky took a deep breath. Her biggest obstacle wasn't Raj, it was Mak. Mak had created a cult of personality here. "Yes, it is what Mak would have wanted," she started. "And I have no doubt he could have delivered. But the plain fact is, I can't. *We* can't. But we can honor his memory by accepting the very real impact of his death—by pausing, instead of rushing in as if nothing has happened. A delay isn't failure. We cannot control the regulatory process, but we can control this date. We need to circle the wagons, restore this team, fortify the organization-at-large, repair our vendor relationships, and retool clinical development for the challenges ahead."

"So much for consensus," someone whispered.

Franky acted like she hadn't heard it. She knew there would be plenty of time to show them she meant what she said about consensus and teamwork. Priority one was relieving the company pressure before it blew up in their faces.

| | | | |

"I don't want to get in your way. I want to make things easier for you. I'm here on your invitation."

Franky waited for Raj to respond. It was a minor miracle she had managed to get him out of the lab for lunch, but she suspected even he knew something had to give. She had brought him to a Thai place that was her favorite for potentially explosive interventions because it had tables in the back isolated from other diners. If he lost it, it wouldn't be too embarrassing. As for Franky? She never lost it.

Raj sipped on his glass of iced tea, then silently stared into space.

"Honestly," she continued. "If we work together, we can make this work. We can bring this drug to market. That's what we both want, right?"

He bit into an ice chip, letting the noise linger before answering. "Yes, but sooner rather than later."

"But a rush to clinical trials will crush this team. If mistakes get made and it takes any longer than the current projections—we're finished—at least in our current form."

Raj looked away as the server brought them appetizers.

"If there's one adjective everyone uses to describe you, it's 'brilliant,' Raj."

He turned to face her with the beginnings of a smile. "I'm guessing there's another one. 'Impossible,' maybe?"

*Unbelievable. Did Raj just make a joke at his own expense?*

"Oh, no, not at all." She allowed a bit of warmth to infuse her sarcasm.

"Yeah, right."

"Look, I know I can't do this without you." Franky took a spring roll off the plate, passing it to him. "You and Mak started this company. I gave you the resources, but you two gave it a heart and soul. But it did take two of you. I am not replacing Mak. I'm just trying to pick up the slack. Maybe if you let me do what I do, you'll like what happens. Maybe we won't need more meetings like this. But, please just give me the chance."

Raj declined the spring rolls plate, instead taking a long pull from his drink, swishing iced tea between his teeth like mouthwash. "I've got nothing to say about that. Lily already gave you the chance when she gave you her vote."

"It isn't going to work though, if we aren't working together."

He swallowed. "Message received."

| | | | |

Over the next few days, Franky held one-on-ones with her senior staff and some leaders beneath them. Lauren had some of the most serious complaints. She sounded alarm bells left and right about Raj's outright refusal to deal with invoice reviews, budgets and forecasts.

"We could lose valuable vendors," she said, anger flushing her face. "By the way, that includes a major third-party manufacturer we are completely dependent on to succeed. And I don't blame them. I don't. They weren't being paid, Franky."

Franky started to react but chose to listen instead.

"And, as you know from being on the receiving end, it completely hinders my ability to project expenses. It's crazy. It's unprofessional. It's untenable!"

Franky kept nodding so much she felt like a marionette by the time Lauren showed her the litany of overdue accounts she had tracked down thus far.

"Look. Raj may want to save the world, and that's great. More power to him. But Techular is still a business. And businesses are rooted in the numbers. You get it, of course. You know what I mean."

Franky nodded. *More than you know. This is serious stuff. And it looks like my CFO may walk if things don't improve. Though it's also curious why she didn't take action herself. Why isn't her team receiving and processing the invoices directly? Why aren't they devising better systems? You have to be like water and go around the rocks, particularly when those rocks own the company.*

Her next stop was with Larry to get a better sense of the state of human resources. Larry had a more sophisticated and holistic view of the organization than the rest of the executive team, particularly regarding the cultural decline.

She instantly liked Larry. He knew his stuff and seemed to be trying to put systems and processes in place. Also, it didn't hurt that his assessment of the executive team and Techular as a whole matched Franky's. He wasn't blameless in the dynamic that had taken hold at Techular, but he seemed to own his share of the dysfunction. She sensed he would be a good thought partner. He was professional and direct, even about his eyes wandering toward the exit at times.

"Don't get me wrong. I still want to be a part of this success. *Most* of the time. But there are more days than not lately when I feel my conviction waning."

Larry didn't deliver this news in a vindictive fashion, but as a matter of fact, making Franky realize his threat was grounded in reality, whether she liked it or not. More troubling, the more Larry talked, the more she realized how deep and fragile the people problem was.

"Still, I'm hopeful you'll turn this all around," Larry added before summing up his critique. "It's not just Raj. We have problems all over the place, really. While Mak was still here, everyone basically felt like he was their boss—even if someone had been placed between them. So, now they are facing the reality that they actually do have a boss who isn't Mak and they don't like it. A lot of Steve's problems will improve as his team finally engages in some real work. But, the retention problems with the research and development staff are likely to continue. Raj treats his best, most senior people like junior lab techs. Who can blame them for leaving?"

"Really, it's that bad?"

"Oh yeah, high-level scientists are shut out of his process. Instead, he assigns them to menial tasks, insulting to their expertise and their dignity."

"Yikes, I figured we had some culture/climate issues in the labs given Raj's temperament, but I assumed the biggest problem was going to be getting other departments more integrated. I didn't realize he was pushing away his own staff, too."

"Oh yeah. It's bad. We've got a real brain drain problem. We've already lost top talent because of his need to do everything himself. He was able to pull Dr. Warren onto the team, but I am not sure how long he'll stay given Raj's style."

"That is a problem."

Larry started to get up. "Oh, it's a problem, all right. And every person who leaves takes with them valuable knowledge. And the bad press makes it tougher to replace them."

Then there was Steve, the chief quality officer. Steve was sharp and experienced. He was the MD to Raj's PhDs. He would play a leading role in the clinical trials. His first step, referred to as Phase I, would be demonstrating their treatment was safe in healthy humans at the proposed dosing levels.

When Franky had first met him two or three years back, he had struck her as a "can't we all just get along," kind of guy. Quiet and exacting, yet team oriented. He seemed different. The last few years had been hard on him.

"I believe in rules, Franky. If I didn't, I'd be bad at my job. Thanks to Raj, however, I haven't been able to do that job. I'm dead weight. It's good you delayed the trials because, right now, there is no way we could survive them. But I hope you understand this is just a stopgap measure. He's impossible. Something has to change."

Steve paused to give her a what-are-you-gonna-do-about-it look.

She counted to five before responding. "Steve, I keep hearing the same story again and again. Raj is not responding to what others need from him. Things obviously must change. All I'm asking is for you to re-engage and give me time to work with him."

"Oh, I'm willing. I would have left this morning if I wasn't. I didn't like being the one who drew your ire, but I understand why you said what you did. I just don't think you know what you're up against."

"Truthfully, I didn't. But I am starting to. I've had the same headache since Monday. Now it's Friday."

He laughed, revealing something more akin to sympathy than she had received from the others. "I think I've had the same one since—since before the accident."

She lost him for a second as he no doubt relived the experience once again in his mind.

Then, his expression turned serious again. "Look, I know you've got a lot of pressure on you and I'll help you any way I can. But the Raj situation has to be addressed one way or the other. We can only put up with this kind of willful dysfunction for so long.

*Willful dysfunction. Good choice of words.*

# CHAPTER FIVE

# THE
# MATCHMAKER

It was Friday, quitting time. The weekend at last. Larry could finally breathe. As he closed down his computer and grabbed his things, he could feel himself relaxing. He pictured himself binge-watching TV with his phone on airplane mode, totally disconnected from the maelstrom at work he had been enduring for months. Or was it years?

As he switched off his floor lamp, the phone on his desk rang. He started for the door, convinced it could wait until Monday. Before rounding the corner, he looked back at the blinking lights and sighed. *Maybe I should get that.*

|||||

Larry wasn't sure if he was relieved to see Franky still in the parking lot lowering the drop-top to her vintage Mustang convertible. On one hand, he was glad he didn't have to call her at home. On the other, he didn't relish ruining someone else's weekend, too.

*Oh, well,* Larry thought. *She would want to know sooner rather than later.*

Larry approached her car. She cut the engine with a twist of her wrist.

"We got bad news," he said.

"I guess my glass of cabernet is going to need to wait."

Larry nodded. "Should I get right to it or should we have a moment of silence for the weekend that just died?"

||||| 

"When?" She asked Larry as they walked back through the doors.

"Earlier today, evidently."

"How many went with him?"

"Two for the moment, but there could be more," said Larry. "But the real problem is bigger than that. Dr. Warren is highly respected, not just here, but around the world. It was a bit of a surprise when Raj landed him—and not just because he didn't tell the rest of us—but it was real coup to have him aboard. We sent out press releases, etcetera. Franky, he's only been here a few months."

"Great, that's all we need. *More* people bad-mouthing us while we make our way through Phase 1 of the trials. Do we know any details?"

"Well, according to Steve, Raj was berating Dr. Warren in front of the team. Again. But the reality is, this was just the last straw. He's a world-renowned expert in his field, yet Raj wouldn't give him any autonomy or authority. Of course, the man quit. I probably would have done the same thing."

"What did Raj have to say for himself? After all, this was his hire."

"I'll let you know as soon as he tells me." Franky's eyes widened. "Yeah, that's right. He hasn't even informed me yet. No notice when he hires him. No notice when he quits. I only found out from Steve, who heard it from one of his managers who happened to be in the lab when it all went down." Larry paused and drew a deep breath. "Sorry, I'm not helping. I'm just at my wit's end here. I was about to leave but now I have to make sure he and the two others are properly terminated. We need to revoke all physical and cyber systems access, etcetera. Raj didn't bother to tell anyone, so none of this got done."

"This is a nightmare. And not just because of the admin headaches."

Larry stopped to look her in the eyes. "Franky, you've been on the inside for six months now. And we've made remarkable progress as a team. The trials have finally started, our monthly projections are on the nose, but . . ."

"I'm with you. Raj has seemingly accepted my presence and occasionally, he follows through with my suggestions. But, to your point, I just don't know if it's enough. If he's going to be our chief scientific officer, he needs to change his attitude towards people . . . and collaboration in general. He needs to lead! Or . . ."

"Or what?" Larry asked.

"Uh, I . . . I don't know. We have to do *something*. I am not willing to throw in the towel, but my bag of tricks is empty. He's a one-third owner and the brains—we literally don't have anything without him. We can't get rid of him. He practically *is* the product."

Larry interjected, "Maybe we need to call a professional?"

"A psychiatrist?" Franky joked. She looked like she instantly regretted it. "Sorry, what are you talking about?"

Larry chuckled, "No, I *was* thinking of something more like a coach."

"A coach? Are you crazy? Feels like throwing good money after bad. Coaching these days is an honor. It's an investment. Something you do for your best, most capable . . . " Franky stopped herself. She put her head in her hands and rubbed her temples. "Actually, Larry, I don't know why I'm fighting you on this. What choice do we have? What other lever do we have to pull? It's clear I can't help him. I give up. I am all-in."

*Raj and an executive coach. This is a sitcom waiting to happen—only I'm not sure I won't be contributing to the laugh track. . . . Ugh, this has to work or we're sunk.*

| | | | |

If Lake Elliot couldn't do it, nobody could. Larry excitedly hurried to the reception area, where Lake was waiting. He had unsuccessfully pitched coaching for Raj about half a dozen times under Mak's leadership. Mak, of course, wouldn't hear of it.

Larry was drawn to Mak—just like everyone else. Unlike the rest of the crew, however, he had always been worried about the impact that Mak's charismatic style had on the team. There never seemed to be a problem too big for Mak to tackle . . . with his personality alone.

Larry would have never wished Mak away. And certainly not dead. But there was no denying Franky was a substantially better leader . . . and a *better partner* to work with. She truly believed in strong teams and often preferred the solutions of others to her own.

The last place Larry worked, where he was essentially the second-in-command of HR, he had witnessed what he considered a minor miracle. His job had opened up because his boss, Courtney, had just been promoted and they needed someone to take her former position. Larry had hit it off with Courtney and got the gig.

The only problem? It was Courtney's first real executive leadership role and she, like Raj, had no idea what she was doing. I mean, she knew HR inside and out. And she even knew a lot about leadership. She just didn't know much about leading at the enterprise level—and earning a seat at the table with the executive team. However, *unlike* Raj, she saw her own talent gap and brought a coach in to help close it. It was one of the most admirable things Larry had ever witnessed. He wasn't sure, but he suspected she paid for the coaching out of her own pocket. *Now, that was owning the problem—and the solution.*

Almost immediately, Courtney remastered her entire calendar to prioritize executive engagement with the company's business unit leaders and departmental planning with the HR team. The whole organization changed after that. Courtney earned her seat at the table and HR became a powerful enabler.

Not many people knew there was a coach behind Courtney's transformation, but Larry did, and he kept the coach's information on file. Just in case. As in, *break glass in case of emergency*. Well, they were officially in emergency territory now.

As Larry approached reception, he spotted Lake sitting in a comfortable lounge chair, making a note on his tablet. Lake had longish, wavy hair. He wore a suit and no tie. Larry instantly remembered how Lake carried himself with low-key authority. You felt like the man knew his stuff, yet at the same time, he never lorded it over anyone.

If Lake failed to make a dent in Raj's psychic armor, everybody would be disappointed, but nobody would blame him. It would just confirm a fact everyone already took for granted: Raj was hopeless. However, if Lake actually made some progress with the "mad scientist" (Larry's pet name for Raj), then Larry finally would be able to build some semblance of the leadership culture that was missing in their largest department.

| | | | |

Larry rapped on the partially open door. "Franky?"

Franky, who was going through what looked like financials, looked up from her well-organized desk. She gave Larry a big smile. She always made an effort to exude warmth and inclusion to everyone in the office, right down to the guy in shipping. It was smart. It didn't just win her personality points . . . it built trust, the kind of trust that opened up the lines of communication, particularly when news was bad. It was just unfortunate these days there was so much of it.

Larry motioned to Lake, standing behind him. "This is Lake Elliot. The executive coach I was telling you about."

"Oh, sure, come on in." She stood to shake Lake's outstretched hand as the two entered. "Have a seat. Can I get you some water? Coffee?"

"We may all be in the mood for something stronger here in a minute," joked Larry.

"No, thanks." Lake smiled at Larry's ice breaker. "I'm fine."

Larry turned and shut the door. It closed a little too loudly, causing Franky and Lake to jump a little. "Sorry, it got away from me a bit there."

Franky motioned for Larry and Lake to take seats in the simple but comfortable chairs in front of her. As they sat, Lake eyeballed the art hanging on her office walls. It featured what looked like clocks made of dripping wax.

"You're a Dali fan?" Lake asked, as he flipped open the leather folio protecting his tablet.

"I might seem like I'm all business, but I was actually an art minor with a love of surrealism."

"I'm a surrealism fan, too," said Lake. "I mean, I don't own a Lobster Telephone or anything."

As Franky and Lake shared a laugh, Larry figured this must be some art world inside joke. He made a mental note to Google "lobster phone" when he got out of this meeting. Still, to stay relevant, he pointed to the picture of the deformed clocks and said, "Either way, we can all agree that time is slipping away."

"Yes. Yes."

"Franky, as I told you," Larry continued, "Lake here worked with an executive over at InTech for about a year. He was amazing. I experienced the results firsthand. Totally turned around the situation . . . and not just with the employees of the leader in question, but with her peers, too. He's a miracle worker."

"I think he may have to be in this case," Franky added.

"Well, I don't know about miracles. The only water I ever walked on was frozen solid," said Lake. "Anyway, I am not exaggerating when I say I don't *do* anything, the *doing* is in my client's domain. I explore the situation with them. Then we clarify a path forward. I support them through the transformation. And, I make sure they are set on the path to mastery. But the hard work, the doing, is all on them."

"Sounds like a nice way of saying you aren't responsible for your client's failures," Franky said with a pugilistic smile. Larry's heart sunk. He hoped Franky's mind wasn't closing to the opportunity already.

"That is one side of the coin, I suppose. But I prefer to think of it as not robbing them of their hard-earned successes." Lake responded confidently.

"Fair enough," she said, holding her smile.

"So, why, exactly, am I here?"

"Uh oh, Larry didn't fill you in on our challenge?"

Larry jumped in, laughing a little under his breath, "Oh, I told him."

"I like to hear the same story from multiple perspectives, if that's okay with you."

"Sure, no problem, I just wasn't sure how much background to give you," Franky replied.

"Our Chief Scientific Officer Raj Patel is the reason you're here," said Franky, taking the lead. "My private equity firm and I helped start the company with Raj and Mak Reddy about seven years ago. For the first six years, I was essentially a silent partner. My firm wrote the checks. Mak led the company and Raj led the science. Unfortunately, Mak died in a horrible accident about a year ago. Even more unfortunately, Mak was the glue that held everything together. *Everything.* Of course, there is no product without Raj, but without Mak, there was no company, no organization. While the company was imploding, Raj threw himself into his work. He isolated himself from the executive team and his own people. Meanwhile, I tried to bring in an outside CEO but failed to win over Raj—or Mak's daughter and heir, Lily. Then, about six months ago, I stopped making suggestions and made a commitment to lead . . . and so here I am."

"Can I interrupt you there?" Lake asked politely.

"Please."

"How did Raj respond to you taking over? Did he see the merits?"

"Yes and no. Actually, it was his idea. I just ran with it. Or, I guess it would be more accurate to say, I called his bluff. I ambushed him at dinner with a CEO candidate because he wouldn't take my calls and he went apoplectic. He basically accused me of watching the company fail without lifting a finger to help, challenging my silent partner status through all of the strife. The next day I convinced Lily to support me as the successor to her father."

"Yikes. And how did he respond to that?"

"Not well, as you might expect. He's tolerating me, though. He's even reluctantly taken some of my advice regarding the leadership team and his own department—but not in a way that would give it a chance. He just has such poor people instincts and skills."

"What do you mean?"

"Well," said Larry. "We tend to call him the mad genius because he's brilliant, but he gets frustrated or angry when he has to deal with 'common folk' and do the types of everyday activities expected of someone in his leadership role."

"Or maybe he's just incapable of connecting and cooperating with others," said Franky. "I'm not sure which. For instance, I told him he needs to meet with his team—so he held a meeting. He didn't have a real agenda or purpose, so both he and his team considered it a waste of time. After that, they just went back to work."

"A lot of it is his personality," Larry added. "He's intellectually gifted but lacking in emotional intelligence."

"Right. He trusted Mak to be the people person, the nation builder. They were best friends and Mak would usually win him over or wear him down. They had a lot of history. He would follow Mak's lead. Everyone else?" Franky shrugged. "Not so much."

"How is this affecting the operation?"

Larry broke in, "Well, now that Franky's here, we've contained a lot of the problem to the labs. But we're losing talent. Just recently, Dr. Warren split after being subjected to too much of the Raj treatment. Two others left with him and we are concerned a few more may follow once they land."

"Right. I read about that in the *Times*."

Larry and Franky shared a look.

"That's exactly the kind of press we don't need," said Larry. "Worse, if this continues, we're going to end up with a group of seriously junior yes-men and women under him, which means everything will just start and stop with Raj. We are just getting too big for that."

"Larry hit the nail on the head. We've made a lot of progress. I am really proud of the broader team. It is really maturing. But I just don't know what to do with Raj. He needs to change, and I don't know how to create that change. Several of the levers I usually have at my disposal are missing. While on paper he reports to me, he's also an owner, I can't fire him or even use that as an unspoken threat. It is a very sticky situation. Which is why you're here."

"And then, there's Steve," Larry said pointedly. "He's probably the most pissed off of anybody here."

"Steve's our quality officer," explained Franky. "Someone else Raj routinely keeps out of the loop, even though he can't succeed without him. The most basic way of saying it is: Raj is the scientist and Steve is the medical doctor. We can't get through the trials without the right hand offs and protocols between their teams. I've encouraged Steve to be more aggressive in his attempts to partner—he had all but disengaged. But *everyone* is getting tired of working harder than Raj at the collaboration part. At some point, you just can't take it anymore. We need to either rip down the walls between team members or go home. I mean, if we don't succeed, it won't matter how amazing this treatment turns out to be because no human will ever be allowed to buy it."

Lake looked up from his notes. "Has Raj always been like this?"

"Great question. Larry's had a much better view for much longer than I. Larry, what would you say?"

"He's definitely worse than before. Mak managed to get what we needed out of him. He loosened him up. Now that he's on his own, Raj thinks he only has to answer to himself. Worse, I don't think he's been sleeping regularly. The fact that he's not taking care of himself means he's in bad shape to deal with everything else coming at him."

"So Mak's absence has really affected the man from a personal perspective?"

Larry sighed. "They had been best friends since graduate school. But, even if Mak were still alive, we would have a problem due to our size and the added pressure of the clinical trials. I actually suggested bringing in a coach before, but Mak didn't think it was necessary. In the meantime, our organization has grown. A lot. When we were just a few dozen people, we needed our chief scientific officer in the lab. But now we need a CSO who can step away from the bench, lead more, and do less."

"You're not wrong, Larry. Everything you've said so far is a fair assessment. Raj was never a people person but now he's almost a recluse. And his failure to engage is making him the company pariah," Franky added.

"Well, let's get to the bottom line, then. What does success look like?" asked Lake. "What would be the ideal but realistic situation in your minds?"

Franky considered Lake's question for a few moments. "We can't work around Raj. His role is too integral to running an efficient, safe, and ultimately successful operation. But then again, he can't fulfill his responsibilities until he becomes more communicative and collaborative. He has to build a team, not just in the lab, but across the organization. He needs to be more sensitive to . . . to *people* issues. He has to be a leader, an integrator, and again, not just within *his* team, but across senior management as well."

Larry nodded, then said, "Mak led *for* Raj all those years. But he didn't do him any favors. Raj never had to develop the kind of instincts and emotional intelligence other leaders in his position do. Everything just fell into place around him, leaving him with the mistaken impression that's how it works, that organizations just form magically around you and take care of themselves."

"I've talked to him until I was blue in the face," Franky put in. "I don't know how to get him to where he needs to be. Maybe you do?"

*Okay, Lake, time to deliver some words of wisdom. She's giving you your shot. Take it!*

"Okay, so let me repeat back some of the things you've told me to make sure I've got it right. Raj always possessed these tendencies, but Mak had a regulating effect on him and the whole team. Since Mak's been gone, Raj has gotten markedly worse and the team has grown more impatient. Meanwhile, He doesn't understand the basic need for leadership, let alone know how to do it so he hasn't developed any of the systems and processes that might pull his team or the organization together. His people are frustrated, and many have started to show it with their feet, walking out the door. The executive team is furious to the point where he has little credibility in their eyes (despite being the brains of the operation). And Franky, you've tried to coach him and he's taken some action, but awkwardly, resulting in him reverting back to his old ways almost immediately."

Franky nodded, "You've got it. Outwardly, he's acting a bit more cooperatively. But he's not doing enough to turn the ship around."

"Does Raj know you were thinking of bringing in a coach? And if so, how did he respond?"

"I don't think he knows about you." Larry looked at his boss, "Franky?"

"Actually, I did mention it to him," she replied. "He didn't react. But, then again, I could have been saying the sun had pulled out of its orbit and was hurtling toward the earth and I think I would've gotten the same nonresponse."

Larry couldn't help but laugh. "It would help the situation if other people thought he was trying. We all know there is nothing Raj cares more about than getting this drug to market. And yet, we can't get him to act as if he actually understands what it will take," said Larry. "Some of the easiest stuff we ask him to do, he only obliges grudgingly, as if he's doing us a favor instead of helping his own business succeed. And when he has a staff meeting or shows up to one of ours . . . well, like Franky said, it's almost always a disaster. He doesn't know what to say. Meanwhile, everyone is either too eager to agree with him—or too angry to constructively engage, depending on the audience. So, he avoids."

Lake finished up whatever he was writing, then put the pad and pen back in his satchel. "It's a shame. Raj has a lot to offer, obviously."

*What are you doing? Why is your pen going away? That's it? Give us some hope here, buddy.*

"So, what do we do?" Larry asked anxiously. "There *is* something we can do, right?"

"With your permission, I'd like to speak to Raj. Today, if he's available."

"Well, he's here," said Franky uncertainly. "And I'm pretty sure he'll talk to you if I ask him to. He just may not be very—"

"Nice," said Larry, finishing her thought.

"Right," said Franky. "But, seriously, he's not a bad guy, so I wouldn't give up. I mean, he just has a certain way of thinking, so . . ."

"I'm sure our conversation will be unwelcome on many levels, particularly if we find him tunneled into something critical. But, actually, that will be kind of helpful in its own way," said Lake.

"How so?"

"Seeing Raj agitated will draw out some of the problematic behaviors you've been describing. I need to see and hear what he is struggling with before I can propose a strategy. It's about finding a viable way to reframe how Raj perceives this situation and his role in moving it forward. How does he see the challenge? What does the work of leading look like to him?" He turned to Franky. "After I get his take on all this, I'd like to talk to you, alone, if that's okay. No offense, Larry, I just . . ."

Larry broke in to avoid the need for whatever Lake was going to say next, "Please, please. None taken. You two—no, you *three*, including Raj, have some delicate details to work out. I am just happy to have helped with the matchmaking."

*I've got my fingers crossed for you, and a few toes!*

CHAPTER SIX

# THE
# COACH

*What am I walking into?*

Lake wondered just what his meeting with Raj would entail, considering all the horror stories everyone had just fed him. He always found it interesting how different his assessments were from those of the people who hired him. Frequently, he found their beliefs seemed to create a mythos about a person which often over-reached reality.

Lake knew subject-matter experts such as Raj often made the most powerful leaders because they knew the work and the culture inside and out. Yet the journey to leadership for them can often be devilishly hard, always pulling them away from what they love most: the technical work.

Many people think of raw intelligence and focus when they think about experts like Raj. But Lake had grown accustomed to thinking about the other side of the coin. *What is the price of hyper focus and brilliance?* A narrowed passion on *one* thing frequently comes at the detriment of quite a lot of other things. From the stories he had heard from Franky and Larry, Raj was a prime example of this phenomenon.

*Raj, my friend, just how much of the world have you been blocking?*

Security escorted Lake through the corridor. He learned Raj

71

had an office in the executive suites beside Franky, but rarely used it. Instead, Raj favored a converted conference room overlooking his lab. As Lake made his way toward it, he noticed Raj's door was ever so slightly ajar, as if to say, "You can bother me if you need to, but you shouldn't."

Approaching, Lake felt like a gunslinger in one of those black-and-white Westerns his father used to watch, headed for a showdown with a dangerous outlaw—one with a reputation for a fast hand. It was a bad analogy since he wasn't looking for a fight, but his presence was going to be frustrating to someone who felt cornered and alone.

Lake knew his only shot at a breakthrough was seeing events through Raj's eyes. He quickly reorganized the facts he had collected, mentally transporting from Larry and Franky's perspective to Raj's. As he neared the door, Lake pretended to be Raj . . . in his own mind.

*"You people betrayed me,"* Lake said to himself as Raj. *"I started this company. You are here because of my work. Mak was just a boss to you, but I lost my best friend. Now my remaining partner has engineered a coup. How dare she!"*

As Lake opened the door to Raj's office, he noticed the entire right-hand wall was made of glass, creating a fishbowl effect. It allowed Raj to see directly into the lab from his perch. But it also did the reverse, allowing the occupants of the lab to see straight into Raj's office. Lake sensed the nearby researchers' eyes watching him.

*Did all those people know who he was and why he was here? Maybe.* Small companies were like small towns—everybody knew each other's business.

Raj looked up from some printouts he was studying. "Can I help you?"

"Yes, Dr. Patel, I'm Lake Elliot. I think you were told I would be stopping by?"

"Yes. Yes. Franky's assistant gave me a heads-up."

Raj coldly stared at Lake a moment. Expressionless.

"Well . . . mind if we talk?"

Raj exhaled, pushed his papers aside and waved Lake in. His smile was strained, his body language less than welcoming. He crossed his arms as he leaned back in his chair—showing equal signs of skepticism and resentment.

Picking up on Raj's cues, Lake gave him an out, "If this is a bad time . . ."

"Any time is a bad."

"I can only imagine. I appreciate you giving me a few minutes." Lake shut the door behind him. "Okay if I sit?"

Raj responded with some combination of a shrug and a nod.

Lake suddenly noticed there *was* no place to sit. Both chairs in front of Raj's desk had stacks of papers, journals, and other items piled atop them. They went nicely with the other scattered stacks of papers. *How long had all this stuff been accumulating?*

Picking up a pile occupying one of the chairs, Lake placed it on an empty space on the floor.

"Sorry about that. We've been busy around here."

"No worries." Lake settled into the chair. "First, I just wanted to express my deepest sympathies—I can't imagine dealing with the totality of the circumstances you find yourself in."

"And what circumstances are you referring to?"

"I mean dealing with your best friend's passing and the loss of control over the business you two created, for starters. I've heard about how you were inspired to figure out this disease in the first place and how you and Mak left the security of your jobs for your mission. You certainly both put your hearts and souls into this effort. I know you will find success, but I am truly sorry you're having to go it alone."

The statement seemed to get Raj's attention. "It's been very difficult, but, as Mak always said, 'Ever forward.'"

"So, how much do you know about who I am and what I do?"

"I have a vague idea. You're a life coach or something like that. Truthfully, I don't know much about it. I didn't request the help."

"Okay, no big deal, a vague idea is better than none. I am an executive coach, not a life coach. There is a bit of a difference. Life coaches focus on success and satisfaction with your life. In contrast, you could say an executive coach focuses on success and satisfaction in your career. So, with that in mind, why am I here?"

"Seriously?" Raj wrapped his arms closer to his chest. "Well, after spending the morning with Franky, I would think you already know why you're here without me having to go through the embarrassment of weighing in."

"That's fair." Lake shifted in his seat as he formulated his response. "Perhaps, I chose my words poorly. Let me ask my question another way. Would you mind giving me *your* perspective on why I'm here?"

Raj uncrossed his arms and leaned forward. "You want the truth? I'll give you the truth. You're here because my partner, the self-appointed CEO, doesn't want to deal with me anymore. I thought perhaps she was going to stick it out, but now it appears she has sent someone else to do the job."

"What job is that?"

"To 'fix' me, I suppose."

"What does that even mean? Are you broken?"

"Yes. Well, that seems to be the overall opinion. Franky came rushing in to 'save' everybody, but she didn't realize the problems I was facing. I could have just stayed home and mourned Mak or held a bunch of meetings with the executives. Instead, I poured every ounce of myself into getting us to the trials, getting us to market. And my reward was a collective vote of no confidence. She might not have told you, but she went around me to Mak's grieving daughter . . . just minutes after he was laid to rest. Minutes! I wasn't even included in the discussion. It was humiliating having these people conspiring behind my back, like I'm some problem child who won't behave. Someone who needs to be 'fixed.'"

Lake nodded. *Raj doesn't just feel betrayed. He also feels abandoned—by his mother, by his best friend, and now by the only person he thought might be able to help him through this.*

"Once more I find myself left out of the discussion again."

"You do?" asked Lake.

"Yes. I wasn't asked if I wanted a coach, one was hired for me. And here you are."

"First, thank you."

"*Thank you?* Thank you for what? Being resentful?"

"For being so open and honest. For being willing to expose more than a few raw nerves. I asked you for the real story and you gave it to me. But I do want to make something clear, I haven't been hired. Not yet. The purpose of my conversations with you and Franky is to understand the situation, to get a sense for the people involved, and to form an opinion as to whether I can actually add value."

"That's beside the point. All I know is nobody, including Franky, wants to deal with me or what I feel is best for this company. Which is also funny, because, as I said, I do the real work here. My work is the sole reason for Techular's existence and will be the sole reason for its ultimate success. Now, I know that sounds like narcissism but it's not—it's a fact. Which is why I'm all about trying to move forward with my work. The problems they are working on in the executive offices are all easily solvable. I am trying to solve problems that no other person on the planet has solved. And, that work is not going to get done by having a lot of useless meetings with people who do not possess the training or the skills to help."

Raj stared coldly at Lake, reflecting just how pissed he really was.

"Okay, fair enough," Lake said mildly. "Franky's been here a while now, right?"

"Six months, but I have known her for years."

"You two haven't developed any kind of relationship or rapport?"

"I have accepted her existence."

"I'm sure she appreciates that," Lake said, laughing.

"You're laughing but I didn't mean it sarcastically. Sometimes my choice of words is not the best. What I mean is I'm still angry, but I'm not hateful. She did go behind my back but that's not the whole story. I challenged her to do more than just complain and she took me up on it. I'm still angry about how she did it; but she has had a positive impact. She is doing the job better than I. I'm not blind to that."

Raj paused as his steely gaze softened. "I'll be honest with you. I am sorry. What's your name again?"

"Lake. Lake Elliott."

"Lake, here's the thing. I was not in good shape after Mak died. I did exactly what I did when my mother passed. I poured myself into my work. I ignored everything else around me. I focused on the work and not the team. This is my nature anyway—but it was twice as bad as I have ever been. I have never been very good with people, particularly groups of them. Mak always took care of that sort of thing. After he was gone, the worse things got, the less time I spent dealing with them. I know I made a lot of people angry. It made me angry, too. I decided to just focus on the problems I had a chance at solving."

Lake was relieved to hear Raj tell the story this way. It showed more self-awareness than the team was giving him credit for. "That sounds terrible."

"Now, I'm angry. The management team is angry, and my response is to . . . ."

Lake finished his sentence. "Throw yourself back into the work?"

"Exactly."

"Doom Loop," Lake nodded knowingly.

"What?"

"It's what Jim Collins, the guy who wrote a book called, *Good to Great*, referred to as a reinforcing cycle in which all of the inputs and outputs worsen the situation."

"Oh, a positive feedback loop, you mean. That's what we call it when the product of a process moves the system further away from equilibrium, versus a negative or self-regulating system."

"Yes, that's exactly what it is." Lake smiled again. "Except calling it a positive feedback loop, sounds, well, too positive."

"I see how that could get confusing in this context." Raj nodded. His face seemed to suggest he had made a hidden connection he wasn't willing to share. Instead, he said, "Perhaps, you are already adding value."

Lake decided it wasn't yet time to press Raj on what value he meant. He considered it a win Raj mentioned it at all. "Could you tell me more about your interactions with Franky? And again, be as candid as possible."

Raj sighed and looked away.

"I'm just trying to understand the dynamics."

"The dynamics? Here are the dynamics. Franky thinks I put too much focus on the science. She thinks I should delegate more and do less. She tells me I have to connect better with my people. With other departments. Show more leadership. Well, I think I show plenty of leadership every day. I lead by example." He gestured out his window overlooking the lab. "I delegate plenty. I tell them what to do and they do it. They're doing it now. What more is there?"

"To be fair, Raj, what you're describing sounds more like directing the work than leading the people."

"To be fair, I think that is a distinction without a difference."

"In that case, the two of us could have an interesting debate. Is the purpose of leadership to direct the work? Or is it to do something more, like cultivate strong communities of effort?"

Raj looked like he was about to say something, but changed his mind.

"Okay. Instead of running after that shiny object," Lake said, "I wonder if you could tell me more about what's going on with Steve and clinical development?"

Raj snorted. "Paperwork. Like that matters if we don't have the science right. Look, manufacturing the treatment is all on me. Do you know what that pressure feels like? Of course, we needed to develop patient protocols, but we couldn't do that until the research and development was done. They were trying to put the cart before the horse. They wanted to spend hundreds of hours in meetings and documentation before I could nail down the right production process. It's like I always say, 'Circling a date on the calendar doesn't make it happen.'"

"And how did they respond when you told them why you needed to hold off?"

Everything in the room seemed to stop cold, as if someone had hit pause. There was an uncomfortable silence. Then Raj's face changed. He exhaled sharply. "I didn't know myself, at first. There was nothing to tell. It was more of a feeling . . . so I just let their emails and meeting requests pile up while I probed the issues I could not yet see. Then Mak died at just the same time I finally confirmed the problem and, well, I didn't want to rock the boat while it was sinking. It could have sent everyone over the edge. And, there was just so much work and I was afraid of failure, afraid of letting my mother down, afraid of letting Mak down. I feared I was ruining everything we had built. In the end, it's like I saved the ship, but lost the crew."

"Wow," Lake said softly. "That's a lot of burden for one man to carry."

"Maybe," Raj said, slowly rebuilding the emotional walls that had so unexpectedly crumbled around him. "I carry it because I must. I chose a route and it cannot be undone. This is, as they say, my cross to bear."

Lake leaned back in his chair. He wanted Raj to sit with these feelings but not for too long. After a moment, he broke the silence, "In my experience, the truth almost always lies somewhere between it's all your fault and you didn't have a choice. Taking responsibility for your actions is important. Taking *all* of the responsibility, however, robs others of theirs. It may seem awkward given where we just were, but could we return to your relationship with Franky? It seems important given where you are and what you are both trying to do."

Another sigh from Raj. *Now he seems more perplexed than angry.*

"We're opposites. We don't even speak the same language. We don't have the same understanding of . . . anything. She's tried to help me and I've tried to follow her advice; but what works for her just doesn't work for me."

"Really? Tell me about that."

"When she took over, it was a shock to the system. It woke me up a little. She flew into action across the organization and started making a difference almost immediately. It was the first time I realized Mak's death had maybe affected me more than I realized. It was hard, but I tried not to argue with her. Then she started saying things like, 'Have more team meetings.' So, I did just that. I put meetings on the calendar. She told me, 'Be more communicative.' So, I sent more emails. But nothing seemed to come out of any of it. It was awkward for me and for everyone else. I don't mean to come off as a smartass, but I did do everything she asked me to." He paused and shrugged. "Now, I guess I have to do what you're going to tell me to do."

"Wait. Slow down a minute. So, you don't feel like anything Franky told you to do was helpful to your team? Didn't they appreciate you taking time to talk about how the work was getting done or prioritizing efforts and setting timelines?"

"No. We just stared at each other." He let out a little derisive laugh. "The meetings were the worst. My people just looked at me, wondering what they were supposed to do. And I looked at them, wondering what I was supposed to do. It was a distraction. Waste of time. They already knew what I wanted them to do. Yanking them away from their work to talk about nothing meant nothing got done."

"Okay, I see what you're saying. But you do at least acknowledge you're in an important leadership role here?" Lake asked gently.

"Yes. And again, I am leading. How else would any of the work get done?"

"Right, but I'm just asking if you think the people here need more from you. From what I understand, Mak handled most of the leadership issues when he was here. And your team has grown since then. Do you feel as though you need to improve your skills in that area? I mean, how are your people responding to your efforts? Are they engaged?"

"The way I want them to respond is to do the work. A few haven't wanted to do that. They think I'm asking them do things beneath them and they've left. Which is fine with me. I'm a scientist. I'm not going to sit with them and hold their hands or pander to their egos. There are many qualified people to take their places."

"Don't take this the wrong way, but are you saying your people are dispensable? Interchangeable?"

"No, of course not," Raj snapped back. "That's not what I said."

"Perhaps you feel as if you saved the ship but lost the crew for a reason. It sounds like you repaired the ship but didn't administer aid to the crew . . . and the metaphorical 'battle' injured both."

Raj stared back, not at Lake, but through him. All traces of emotion dropped from his face. He didn't seem angry or defensive. He seemed deep in thought.

After a while, he spoke, "Look, I have two PhDs. Both are in science, not people. Even if I were capable of . . . of administering aid, where would I find the time? The clock is ticking. The work is hard enough and there is still no end in sight. I can either hold meetings or I can figure out how to manufacture this treatment. I can't do both. Could you?"

Raj paused, signaling he didn't want an answer. "Don't respond. I am not an idiot. If that were your perspective, you wouldn't be here. But there's a big difference between what they put in management books and what goes on in the real world. I have had lots of leaders in my career. Not one of them cared about our 'community'—they cared about our *activity* and our *results*."

"Forgive me for saying this, but it sounds like Mak did make the people a priority . . . and Franky does, too."

"Ha, you are so right. Then again, they both left me to do all the work!"

| | | | |

Lake noticed Franky was alone in her office when he returned. He tapped on the glass. Looking up, she signaled for him to enter. Lake closed the door behind him.

Franky could read the seriousness on his face. "Things went that well, huh?" she asked with a nervous laugh.

"I can't coach Raj," Lake said straight out.

"Wait. What?" She shook her head in disbelief. "You're out the door? I didn't see that coming."

"It has to be you."

"What do you think I've been trying and failing to do for the last six months—longer actually?"

"I hear you."

"Do you? Do you really?" She began talking louder and faster as panic set into her face. "Because it sounds like you just told me to get back in the ring after I already took a beating and threw in the towel."

"I can see how it might sound like that, but—"

"Look, I thought I could help him. I really did, but I just don't know how to help someone like Raj. I thought maybe you did, but obviously you don't either. How do you give someone better people skills who doesn't seem to have any emotional intelligence at all? It's impossible."

"Franky, we *can* help him. Together. Here's the thing. If I coach him, there's a 60 percent chance we get him moving in the right direction."

"Sixty? I'll take those odds."

"And," Lake jumped back in, "And, a 100 percent chance he locks you out . . . forever. On the other hand, if you march into his office tomorrow and thank him for meeting with *your* new coach, you two might be able to work this it out and take that journey togeth- er . . . and start healing this organization as a team. I honestly think it's the only way this works. Otherwise, it's a house of cards. We might get Raj leading—sure, but his anger and resentment would prohibit any real positive interactions outside of his own team."

Franky's eyes narrowed. "That was exactly my assessment when I first walked through the door. But in all my years, I've never run into a situation like this, where someone like Raj was so resistant and ill-equipped to lead. I guess I got lucky. All my people were coachable. So, unless you've got another idea to pitch, I think we're done here."

"Franky."

"Yes?" she replied with more than just a trace of frustration.

Lake could tell he was in danger of losing her. "Let me help you."

Franky gasped—or was it a chuckle? "That's what I've been ask- ing you to do. And all I heard was a big fat 'no!'"

Lake spoke as calmly and confidently as he could. "Let me help *you*. I want to coach *you*. I am confident you can get through to him."

"Coach me? How does that help anything? You are *so* not hear- ing me." Franky blurted out, rising up out of her chair.

"Franky," he said softy, pausing to slow the discussion's pace. "I am hearing you. And what I'm hearing *you* say is *you* need help. *You* are frustrated. *You* are in uncharted waters. *Your* ship is sinking. *Your* crew is panicking. *Your* partner is only focused on the boat and the destination. *You* know you can't complete the journey without the crew. I'm hearing what you're saying *and* what you haven't said. My guess is, for the first time in quite a while—maybe in your whole career—*you* sense failure, not land, is on the horizon."

Franky sunk back into her chair. She looked up as if she was going to keep arguing, stopped herself, then took a deep breath.

The room filled with silence. She stared at Lake. He could tell she was sizing him up, wondering if this was an act of some kind? A trick to get out of coaching Raj? Finally, Franky began softly, "What on earth did Raj say to you to make you think this could possibly work?"

"I can't repeat anything Raj said to me in confidence, though we did talk about boats, too," Lake said with a smile. "But, I can give you my observations in the context of what you and Larry shared with me. Raj has only truly connected with a few individuals, ever. And the two he trusted most and knew the longest, have left him. When he started to lose his mother, he threw himself into science to save her. When she passed, he threw himself deeper into it to cope. Then, on the eve of bringing his cure to the world, his partner, his best friend, the man he relied on to keep him connected to everything, died."

"And once again, he threw himself into the work, finding and solving a showstopper while he was at it." Franky chimed in, clearly thinking over what Lake was saying.

"Yes, then, in the midst of reflexively slapping help away, he let his real feelings slip. He cried out to someone he thought might be able to help. Someone who had at least been there from the start. To his surprise, she answered the call. Not quite in the way he was hoping, which made things tough between them. But she has shown her mettle and made real progress, progress not even Raj would deny. Think of the impact of your answering his distress call, of seeing through his anger and rejection and stepping through the door anyway. Think of the complexity of you going around him to gain control but also defending him amidst a clear mutiny. You both humiliated him and made him a hero. Now, given what you've told me about Raj—"

"Stop. Stop. You can stop. I get it. I get it. I can't abandon him. His little bit of trust in me is huge and I can't betray it, or we're done for. He will be alone again and throw himself deeper into the black hole." Franky looked down at her desk, inhaled slowly, then looked back up at Lake. "So, now what? What can I do? I honestly don't know how to help him."

Being careful not to rush things, Lake took the deep breath this time. "That is the right question, but it sounds like a good discussion for our first session. With your permission, I'll get with your assistant on the way out to schedule something."

"Any homework?" she smirked as she stood to shake his hand.

"Franky, if I've read you right, you'll be doing it every waking second between now and our meeting."

Franky laughed. Lake turned to leave.

"There is one thing." He said, looking back at her. "Do make sure to have that conversation with Raj. The sooner the better."

"Any thoughts on the messaging?"

"Just be yourself. Let him know you've decided to hire me for *you*, not him. He needs to know you haven't given up on him."

*Whew. Close one. Of course, there is the little detail of actually delivering on this small miracle. Gulp.*

# CHAPTER SEVEN

# THE

# MENTOR

She couldn't believe she was back where she started. On the car ride home from dinner, she was still in deep thought. Out of the corner of her eye, Franky noticed her husband Gary give her a questioning look.

"I keep thinking about that conversation with the coach we brought in," she said at last. "The one who told me I was the one who needed the coaching."

"Seriously? I can't believe you're still obsessing about that."

"I'm sorry." She sighed. "I am."

"Okay, two things. One: this guy doesn't know you. He doesn't know how big a deal it is that you broke down and called him to begin with. He doesn't understand who you are and what you're capable of. I bet he's used to working with leaders who don't care and who don't know how to coach. And, two: I said it once and I'll say it again—he took one look at Raj and ran in the other direction."

"I wish it were that easy."

"What do you mean?"

"I feel like he does know me. I mean, I spent exactly zero minutes of our conversation talking about myself. Yet he read me like a book."

"Well, he must be some kind of clairvoyant / master manipulator to get you spinning around like this. Exactly, what did he say? How is he supposed to help you?"

"I'm not sure. Lake didn't—"

"Wait. His name is Lake?"

"I told you that."

"Maybe he should go jump in one." Gary took his hands off the wheel to emphasize his joke with air drums.

"Put the bad jokes on hold for just a minute."

"You think my jokes are bad? All these years, you've been lying to me?"

She laughed. "I'm pretty sure I pointed it out on our first date at the Tastee Freez. When you said they should've fired their proofreader. Can we get back to my problem?"

"If we must."

"Lake said if he coaches Raj, it's going to make more problems for me down the road. Raj will think I've given up on him—"

"Which you have." Gary's smile evaporated as he realized how his snarky comment had landed.

She thought for a moment. "I have, haven't I?"

"I didn't mean it like that. You had no choice, considering his inability to understand and relate to other people."

"It's not that I don't agree with you. But you're hearing everything through my filter. Your impressions about Raj come through me. When Lake replayed Raj's story back to me, I wasn't sure which to do first—quit or vomit."

"He didn't put all this at your feet, I hope."

"No, no, not at all."

"Enlighten me then. Broaden my horizons. What did he say?"

"I just think the reason I've been stuck on this for days is because he directed a bright light at a blind spot. I've been partnering with Raj because I'm stuck with him. Until this all went down, I never really thought of myself as in a partnership with him. Mak was the one I trusted to pull this across the line. I mean, I trusted Raj to get the science right and Mak to handle everything else. But, now, without Mak, there's no way around him. It's not that I was being disingenuous in trying to help. But I was forced into it and I didn't trust him. I said some of the right words. But my words didn't match my actions . . . because they didn't reflect how I was really thinking and feeling."

"Okay. So, fill me in then. What story did he tell? Bring me into the circle."

"I think I'm avoiding saying it out loud." Franky paused to let the emotion drain from her throat. "Using the same basic facts I gave him, Lake described a remarkable man who has been scarred by loss, self-imposed isolation, and the betrayal of his partner, a man who desperately needs to reconnect to the people around him to bring a great gift into the world."

Gary put his hand gently on her knee. "I've been on this journey with you. This guy is no picnic. You're not giving yourself enough credit. It's not like you didn't try. You didn't just swoop in and pull the rug out from under him. You tried to help before you ever walked through the door—and after."

"My focus was never on him, not really. I was focused on the people and the treatment. Raj needs my help. He has for a long time. This isn't just one of a thousand problems at Techular—it is *the* problem! Why else am I there if not to solve it? And honestly, what bothers me most is I'm afraid. It's not that I think I gave it my best shot and failed. I didn't and I don't know if my best shot will be enough."

"It sounds like you already know what you must do. You're just working yourself up to do it. Talk it over with this guy. See what he has in mind. It sounds like he might know his stuff. What do you have to lose? He's already climbing around in your head. Let him roam around in there awhile and see what he finds."

She smiled and looked over at him. "Oh, Gary."

"I know. I give and I give without taking."

| | | | |

"Well, let's get down to it."

Franky sat at a table in Lake's conference room, picking at her Waldorf salad through their working lunch. As she chewed a bit of celery and grapes, Franky couldn't help being impressed by the rustic, yet modern suite of offices Lake had set up in San Juan Capistrano. It was only a few miles from Techular but the backdrop of the historical location gave it a decidedly different vibe. His staff seemed sharp and personable. He clearly knew how to hire and develop the right people.

*Maybe I will get something out of this. God, I hope so.*

"Absolutely." Franky said, looking up from her salad, realizing Lake was waiting for a response.

"I was thinking, because of the way everything unfolded during our last meeting, we didn't talk about the process of coaching—at least my process."

"No, we didn't. But I'd prefer to, as you said, 'get down to it.' I have a lot riding on this. And I need results. Like yesterday."

"I'll be brief." Lake cleared his throat as if he were stepping up to the microphone for a speech. "Everything we discuss in this room is essentially meaningless—"

Franky looked up from her salad. "Interesting way to start things off, coach."

"Well, what we do in here is meaningless—or at least, academic, until you give it meaning by taking action."

"I get it. It's not enough to think or talk about action. I must do it."

"Yes, and not just once. There is little we will discuss that'll have an actual impact if it's only carried out once or even twice. Personal proficiency, interpersonal trust, and complex collaboration *all* improve through repetition. That's why coaches create plays and run drills at practice. Because practice doesn't just make perfect for an individual, it tells others what to expect and how to do their part. It helps them anticipate what you're going to do next and collaborate effectively."

Lake continued, "Therefore, in our work together, we will seek to *explore* the current state from multiple angles, *clarify* your plan of action, *transform* your behavior, then *master* the new activity through repetition, continuous improvement and, eventually, mentorship."

"You're making me nervous." Franky said rather forcefully. "You don't seem focused enough on Raj and 'eventually' sounds like a long way off."

"Too true. My focus is on you. If we expect to figure out a new path forward, we need to unpack why you didn't succeed the first time around. We can't skip that part of the process. However, what I can also promise is once we get past that, your path will be clear and you will spring into action. I don't see our work unfolding across months and years—but weeks."

"Okay, it's just that I feel uncharacteristically panicked over this. Work with me here."

"I understand. Just consider, how is this anxiety serving you?"

"W-what do you mean?"

"Sometimes our anxiety pushes us to drive harder than others, to strive for perfection or success they are unwilling to pursue. Other times, it pushes us into action prematurely."

"Well, like the old saying goes, 'Don't just sit there, do something.'"

"Ha. But there's also wisdom in turning that cliché around. I once saw a meditation book titled, *Don't Just Do Something, Sit There*. Consider the possibility your impulses to act may not be serving you well here. We should be as strategic with Raj as you are in business."

"Okay, I'll play nice with your process. Besides, this discussion is just slowing us down even more." Franky said with a wink.

"Great. And remember, what's true for you is true for Raj. You two will need to take your own journey together. Like you, he won't find success at the end of one new thought or action. He will need to *explore* his current state, *clarify* his new framework for leading, *transform* that framework into a methodology, and then *master* it."

Franky sat silently, then laughed under her breath. "So, you're saying I should shut up, be patient, and pay attention because you're teaching me the process I should use with Raj—by using it on me."

"You said it so much better than I did. Except for the 'shut up' part."

"So, what was that process you said again, explore, clarify . . . ?" Franky pushed away her salad and pulled out her notebook. "You used the same words twice so I am assuming they were important."

"I call it the **ECT(M)** Transformation Model. I use it to guide leaders, teams, and organizations through change. I'll include a summary of the model in the information I provide after today's discussion." He watched as she wrote down what he was saying anyway. "As you write out the acronym in your notes, put parentheses around the 'M'. . . "

"Which stands for 'Master?'"

"Yes. You want to make that part of this process conditional on finding success in the 'Transform' phase. In other words, it might take several cycles through the 'ECT' part to hit on the right formula. When that happens, keep going through the first three steps until you find a series of thoughts, words, or actions you want to lock-in and 'Master.'"

Continuing to write in her notebook, Franky said, "I have some questions about how to move someone from 'Clarify' into 'Transform.'"

"Good. You should. That requires real discussion."

# ECT(M)
## TRANSFORMATION MODEL

The **ECT(M)** Transformation Model helps leaders
guide individual, team and organizational development efforts.
The first three phases (Explore, Clarify and Transform)
are often repeated multiple times in succession until the process
and outcomes meet the established criteria.
Then, the last phase (Master) focuses on raising proficiency through
routinization, incremental improvements, and mentoring others.

"But not now?"

"No, not now." Lake flashed an apologetic smile. "The best way to understand how the model works is to experience it. I'd like to start by asking you to describe how our last conversation sat with you. Then I'd like to hear how your conversation with Raj went. Would you mind filling me in?"

"Well . . . to tell you the truth, it didn't sit with me well at all. At first, I questioned your motives for not agreeing to coach Raj. I wondered if you were choosing to work with me because I might be the easier mark—so to speak." Franky paused see how her comment landed. He didn't react, so she continued. "But, fortunately for you—and unfortunately for me—I pushed through those feelings and found some new, more unsettling ones. I realized I was the one trying to dodge Raj. From the beginning, I don't think I was partnering with him for the right reasons or at the right level. My words were decent enough and I did want to help him and the company, but I wasn't seeing things from his perspective. I wasn't getting into his head, trying to help him out of the dark place he'd crawled into. My focus was on rescuing everybody else from what he was doing. He was a perpetrator, not a victim, in my mind. As a result, I didn't do any deep thinking on the matter."

"Perfect."

"Excuse me?"

Lake smiled back. "So long as you aren't kicking yourself too hard, I'm happy you came to this realization."

"Because that's what you were thinking, too?"

"No. It's good because it's helpful given what we're trying to accomplish. When you were thinking you had already done your best thinking on this and consequently tried everything there was to try, it didn't leave a lot of room for re-engagement."

"True. Let's just not celebrate my mistakes too often."

"Never. Just your insights," he said with another smile. "Now, tell me about your talk with Raj. How'd that go?"

"Basically, I told him I needed help turning this team around and had decided to hire you . . . for me. He was taken aback. He said he thought you were there for him. I didn't want him to think I was yanking any support away, so I told him he could still interview some coaches if he wanted to—but I thought it would be best if he chose a partner versus me picking one for him."

"And what did he say to that?"

"He agreed. He said your discussion made him think more favorably about coaching than he had in the past."

"Excellent!"

"Wait, now you *do* want to coach him?"

"No, not me. It still has to be you—but he also has to want it. He has to value it. And it sounds like we're halfway there." Lake paused. It was his turn to write something down. "Let's change gears and get back to you. This next part might sting a bit."

"Oh boy."

"Don't worry, it's nothing you can't handle. The reason it's going to sting is we are going to pick at why your previous attempts failed."

"Okay. Makes sense."

"We've already established your mindset was blocking your best thinking."

"Yep."

"Based on what both you and Raj shared with me last week, that's not the only obstacle."

Franky signed, "I suppose that's good, because I'm still a little lost on what I should actually *do* next."

"Fair enough. The next big problem we must tackle is your difficulty communicating what leadership is and how he should do it."

"Excuse me?" Franky interrupted. This time she did not have a playful smile on her face.

"There's the sting. But bear with me for a minute. Remember, I'm *not* questioning your ability to lead. You do the right stuff for your team and your business. You have amazing people skills. In fact, when I mentioned your name to the stakeholders you had me speak to before today's meeting, they used phrases like, 'She's a natural.' But let's contrast this with what we know about Raj. You've told me many times Raj has poor people skills while being a genius in the more traditional sense. You've mentioned he has excellent knowledge retention and reasoning skills. But you believe he has low emotional intelligence, meaning he has significant difficulty deciphering his own emotions and the emotions of others. This indicates he's frequently frustrated and/or surprised by what's going on inside himself—let alone others."

"Exactly," said Franky, not sure where this was going.

"Even when it comes down to the nitty-gritty parts of the work, this issue is likely to get in the way. What he considers easy, self-evident concepts often intimidate others, requiring considerable explanation. This frustrates Raj even more, causing him to act out, further disenfranchising them. It's a terrible cycle. Now, all of this means Raj is at his most uncomfortable while interfacing or relying on people, particularly if the topic is outside his area of expertise. Why do you think this is?"

"Um, didn't you just say why?"

"I did and I didn't. Think of the moment Raj must interface with another human, let alone *lead* them. He goes from feeling like a global expert to feeling like the village idiot—all in the blink of an eye."

"Harsh." Franky said, a bit shocked by Lake's turn of phrase.

"Make no mistake, I'm not calling him idiot. I am talking about how he *feels* trying to engage others. Imagine what that would *feel* like. Let empathy guide you. It is a powerful tool. Use it to teleport yourself from your vantage point to his. One second, you're at the pinnacle of understanding—the next you're unable to convey that expertise to others or empathize with their struggle to understand. How would that make you feel?"

Franky sat in silence for a bit. "I think I would feel . . . very frustrated and angry. Which is exactly what I see in Raj a lot of the time. I mean, I get it, I'm familiar with emotional intelligence and I know Raj doesn't have it." Franky saw disappointment on Lake's face as she made her comment. "Sorry, I don't mean to be rude. But I do get it. I just don't know how to fix him."

"First, to be clear, we aren't going to 'fix' him because he isn't broken. He is different than you. There is no doubt about that. But Raj is an amazing scientist with a brain uniquely capable to that area of study. What he lacks is an *innate* understanding of people, which has led to avoidance behaviors that compound the problem."

Franky crinkled up her face as she tried to figure out where Lake was going. "So, you're saying he could learn it? If he were to engage more?"

"Yes. The big takeaway about emotional intelligence is it can be developed, versus more stable elements of who we are, like personality or raw intelligence. But I don't believe we should start out trying to develop Raj's emotional intelligence as the immediate goal. First, I think we need to engage him in the *work* of leading. This brings me back to my point about the importance of communicating what leadership is . . . and giving him a clearer sense of how to do it."

"Okay, yeah, we didn't really complete that thought," said Franky.

"What kind of scientist are you? A good one?"

"Come on. I'm not a scientist at all. You know that. I came into my first pharmaceutical gig as a—"

"Could you be, though? If you really wanted to? I mean, do you have the requisite grey matter?"

"Could I do the work? Some of it. But I wouldn't like it much and I wouldn't be great at it. There wouldn't be any Nobel Prizes in my future. Look, I know how this conversation plays out. We each have our talents. We each must play to our strengths. I should respect his contributions more, yada, yada, yada."

"Actually, that's not where I was going. But it is worth saying it seems as if you and Raj have gravitated to professional areas in which you can be excellent given your natural talents—and you both have avoided areas where you're naturally less competent and, therefore, less comfortable."

"Agreed."

"So, since you're alike in this way, how would Raj need to coach you to be a scientist if you suddenly found yourself in the predicament he's in now?"

"You mean if some terrible twist of fate suddenly required me to be a scientist?"

"Yes. Now, be good and play along."

"Well, I would need him to start with the basics. Go light on theory and heavy on practical application."

"And how helpful would it be if he told you the solution to the problem was to just be in the lab more? Spend more time with the equipment? Would that help you? You know absent any real instruction on what to do in the lab and with the equipment?"

Franky laughed. "Obviously, it wouldn't be any help at all."

"Of course not. Yet, when I spoke to you and Raj separately last week, you were both in complete agreement about one piece of the story."

"Well, it's good to hear there was at least one thing we agreed on."

"You both recounted, almost verbatim, the same coaching interactions. You said you told him he needed to communicate more, have more meetings, and so forth. Then, sure enough, when I sat with Raj, he said you told him to communicate more, to have more meetings, and so forth."

"Yes, isn't that pretty straightforward? Don't we both agree he needs to spend less time doing the work and more time connecting with people, delegating, holding them accountable but not doing the actual work, etcetera?"

"For some people, telling them that would have been plenty. But let's consider your assessment of Raj, his discomfort in social situations and his lack of experience with them. Do you think he knew what to do with the people once he got them together? Do you think he talked about prioritizing the work or the work methods? Roles and responsibilities on the team? Do you think he was passing along critical organizational messages they've been missing?"

"But . . ." Franky stopped herself and put her hands over her face, inhaling deeply.

They sat in silence until Lake finally spoke. "That looked like an excruciating, but powerful thought. Tell me about it."

"Why do you do that?"

"Do what?"

"Insist I say it out loud."

"It helps me avoid assumptions about what's going on in your mind. For all I know, you're just getting angry with me for pushing back on you and self-editing to keep yourself from saying something that might damage our relationship." He flashed her a smile to let her know he was indeed picking up on her frustration. "Also, verbalizing it helps you process and reinforce your insights. I promise it's not meant to be patronizing."

"Well, I'm not going to lie. It's a bit uncomfortable."

"Of course, it is. Doing this work is rarely comfortable." He paused, "But I will change up my approach—to avoid being so irritating." Lake laughed at himself under his breath. "Now, would you mind filling me in on the connection you were making?"

"It hit me like a freight train, and it felt so deep when it did. But now it feels almost silly—like, *duh*."

Lake chucked again. "It's funny how that works. One minute's monumental discovery is the next minute's minutia."

"Too true." She paused, considering how to put it. "What I was realizing is that my approach with Raj was almost *dismissive*. On one hand, I was frustrated by his lack of leadership and people skills. On the other, I was giving him advice that presumed he had some understanding of what he was supposed to be doing."

"Boom!"

"There you go again, loving my mistakes!" The two laughed together—a sign some genuine respect and rapport was building between them.

"Someday soon you'll call them insights and we will celebrate them together."

"I'd rather we celebrate my successes."

"Those will come soon enough. But let's step back first. So far, we've established you didn't really partner with Raj deeply enough to see the problem through the right lens—and you didn't intervene in a way that matched up with your own assessment of his capabilities."

"Yes, we seemed to have made great progress establishing why I doomed myself to failure." Franky bowed her head, laughing at herself again. "But no, you're right. I did not match my coaching to his level of understanding. I threw him into the deep end and told him to swim even though he didn't even know what the word meant."

"Good analogy. Look, I know you're anxious to take action and truthfully, like we said earlier, that's crucial. Actually implementing the ideas we talk about is what makes the difference between a productive discussion and a complete waste of time. But—"

"There's always a but!"

"You were born with a lot of innate abilities to understand yourself and others and I suspect those abilities have continued to grow over time."

"Why do I feel another zinger coming on?"

"Yet, the not-so-wonderful part is your natural *feel* for these issues clouds your ability to communicate what you do—and how and why you do it."

"Mostly, I just do what makes sense. I appreciate the compliments underneath the punches, but I just see what needs to be done and do it."

"Exactly. In psychology, they call it unconscious competence. You do what makes sense to *you*. And it works. But someone who doesn't share your raw understanding of people and leadership needs more. Raj needs you to become consciously competent. This is what I was getting at earlier when I criticized your ability to communicate *the work of leading* to Raj."

Lake leaned in and continued, "You can't teach him your feel. You're either born with it or you develop it yourself through repetition. But you can't *teach* it. You inherently know this—and it's why you feel frustrated and hopeless when you try."

"I guess I buy what you are saying. But it's not like I don't know what leadership is or like I've never coached someone before."

"No, of course not. But, up until now you've never encountered someone like Raj."

"Are you saying that all geniuses are this way?"

"Not at all. But most global experts at Raj's level do pay for their competence in one way or another. Think about the time it takes, the focus that's necessary to gain his level of knowledge. It requires an almost obsessive fascination with a small set of subjects. Often, there's quite a lot one must ignore to find the time and bandwidth for that kind of achievement. There are always exceptions to be sure—and it doesn't always impact self-awareness and emotional intelligence—but in general, a person acquiring his level of expertise pays a hefty toll in other areas of their life."

"So experts like Raj shouldn't lead?"

Lake shook his head. "Actually, there is a lot of research suggesting the opposite. Experts actually make amazing leaders since they understand the work and the people who commit their lives to it. But, let's not get lost in a detour that takes us too far from our destination."

"And where is that again?"

"Well, if we can't teach Raj the *feel* of leadership, how do you help engage him in the work so he can develop it on his own?"

"Okay," Franky said, trying to wrap her head around Lake's point.

"Basically, I want to know how you define leadership. Do you have a clear philosophy or framework that helps you explain it to yourself or others?"

"I wouldn't call it a framework exactly, but I definitely have a perspective. I've consumed a lot of the popular leadership literature out there. Take your pick of adjectives in front of the word leadership and I have at least skimmed it: Servant, horizontal, situational, extreme, yada, yada, yada."

"Great, so lay it on me."

"I don't think I'm breaking new ground here, but I think of leadership as the art and science of achieving objectives through others."

"Got it. So, to you, leadership has to do with methods for effectively engaging people in work for the purposes of goal attainment."

"At its base, sure." Franky said reluctantly. "But you don't seem convinced. What's your definition?"

"Let's not abandon yours yet. If it's useful, we should use it. If it's lacking, we should enhance it. How does your definition inform your understanding of the leader's work versus the team's work? In other words, how would sharing this definition with Raj inform the new work he must embrace?"

"Well, truthfully, I'm not sure it does a great job of informing what the new work is . . . but it suggests he should be one step removed from the actual work. I mean, as I think about it, I guess my definition assumes the need to influence others to act in furtherance of a goal—so it also suggests the goals are known and people understand their roles and what to do when." Franky's voice turned up at the end of her sentence, showing a growing lack of confidence in her answer.

"Maybe we should work on something more specific so we aren't implying too much."

"Yeah, I guess my definition is simple but incomplete. It works for me because I have all of this other stuff I add onto it. Now that you have me thinking about it, I'm recognizing it not only misses some of the *what*—the actual work of leading—but also the *how*."

"Tell me more about the *how*."

"Well, my definition leaves out the interpersonal skills and various styles mentioned in all of those leadership books."

"Yes, I suppose it does. That's one of the things I liked about it."

"I take you don't have much respect for leadership gurus then."

"Quite the opposite. My tablet and my bookshelves are full of them. My concern is that jumping to interpersonal skills and leadership styles may make you miss the forest for the trees. Those books are rich with information—but taken together, they weave a complicated tapestry of sometimes conflicting perspectives on how to lead well, versus the basic work of leading."

"So, you think just plain leading is more important than leading well?" Franky asked, unsure how to square Lake's comment with the harm she'd seen poor leaders do.

"I do. I focus on three basic states of leading: not leading, leading, and leading well. In my experience, it is usually far more detrimental when a leader avoids leading. I much prefer it when they engage in the fundamentals, albeit awkwardly or even poorly. I can't think of a single job or sport where it pays to focus on the advanced skills before the fundamentals. And yet, so much of the leadership literature focuses on interpersonal skills and leadership styles—which are more about delivery than the tangible work. But really, I'm more interested in how you think this belief of mine syncs up with your own experiences and, specifically, your opportunity with Raj."

"It's growing on me a little. Actually, it's a simple thought that's hard to disagree with. The hardest question you've asked was on the day we met. You said, 'What does success look like, realistically?' I gave you some kind of meandering answer. But when I imagine Raj succeeding, I don't think it will be pretty or graceful at first—maybe ever. He will need to focus on the fundamentals and just keep repeating them until he builds up his skills and confidence."

Franky sat quietly with her words, taking a few more notes. After a few seconds, she laughed under her breath. "I am sure this isn't a mistake on your part, but I can't help noticing the tie-in between this conversation and what you said earlier about the importance of repetition."

Lake smiled. "Yes, you'll find it'll be a recurring theme with me." Lake shifted in his seat again, signally a change in topic. "Franky, I don't like to begin with my own framework and methodology for a number of reasons. In fact, sometimes I don't even use them. But I would like to share my model with you. *If* you're still interested in my perspective."

"Well, of course I am. I actually like where this talk has taken me. You probably won't be shocked to hear I like the focus on action and consistency."

"Good. I believe it all starts with the purpose of the role. Just think: if we were writing a generic job description for a leader, what would it say? Where would you start?"

Lake paused, waiting for Franky to answer. "Oh, those were real questions? I thought they were rhetorical." She thought for a moment. "Usually, I begin my position descriptions with a summary of the core job functions at the top, then I describe key activities relating to those functions, followed by an explanation of the required skills and / or preferred qualifications at the bottom."

"Me too. That's perfect. By the way, notice how you put the skills toward the end of your list—since they describe how to do the job well, versus what the job is. But, anyhow, let's focus on that executive summary at the top. What are the 'core functions,' as you put it, for the role of *leader*?"

"I guess they would have to define, either collaboratively or by mandate, what the team is for. You know, answer some basic questions such as: What do they do? Why do they do it? How do they do it? What's the strategy? What are the roles? Then I guess, irrespective of the specific answers to those questions, the leader would have to actually turn the crank on the machinery of the team. You know, manage it. And, of course, the leader would need to attend to the results and the people . . . coaching, continuous improvement . . ."

Lake interrupted, "Let me stop you there."

"Did I go astray?"

"Not at all. It was absolutely perfect." He stopped for a second, then went on. "I think you and I are very much aligned. Leadership is a process of social organization meant to yield willing, capable and sustainable communities of effort. As you talked through the job description of a leader, you did a great job of walking through what I call the three domains of leading that naturally follow from this definition. I believe you used the words, 'define, manage and improve.' I say the same thing, using the words, *structure, operate* and *perfect*."

"Wait a second, say that again. I got lost between writing and thinking."

"Ha, fair enough." Lake laughed. "*Leadership* is a process of so-cial organization meant to yield willing, capable, and sustainable communities of effort. *Leading* is the active engagement in the pro-cess of cultivating willing, capable and sustainable communities of effort. *Leaders* are those who accept accountability for cultivating willing, capable and sustainable communities of effort."

# Lead·er·ship

*A process of social organization meant to yield willing, capable, and sustainable communities of effort*

# Lead·ing

*Active engagement in the process of cultivating willing, capable, and sustainable communities of effort*

# Lead·ers

*Those who accept accountability for cultivating willing, capable, and sustainable communities of effort*

"Okay . . . and what was that part about structure?"

"Before we go there, why don't you weigh in on these definitions first."

"Sure. Well, I love the 'communities of effort' part. My definition was goal centric. What I love about this one is it's less about the *ends* and more about the *means*—which makes sense because leading is really about generating the *capacity* to get things done. I think it's a pretty important point, too. When you make leading about goal-achievement, you sort of suggest that leading only occurs in victory, never in defeat. But I can think of plenty of inspirational acts of leading which did not win the day, so to speak; but they all generated powerful communities of effort. Also, I really love the word 'community'. A lot of people would just use the word 'team' in this situation, but 'community' suggests so much more: mutual caring, trust, interdependency, etcetera."

"Yes, exactly! I couldn't have explained it better myself. Now, with all of this in mind, let's return to the work which flows from these definitions. How does one actually cultivate a community of effort? As I said before, my answer is much the same as yours. Essentially, you said—and I am paraphrasing of course—'you need to define, manage and improve it.' Whereas, I say you must: . . ."

Franky finished his sentence for him, "Structure. Operate. Perfect."

"Yes, if a willing *and* capable community of effort is what a leader is trying to create, maintain, and continually improve, it must be *structured*. What are its organizing principles? What is it for? What strategies will be deployed? What work must be done? How should it be done and by whom?" Lake continued, his enthusiasm growing, "It must also be *operated*, right? Simply explaining or even co-creating a community of effort doesn't get the job done. The leader and the community must take action together to run it as intended. What is the tactical plan? How will work be assigned and executed? What stakeholders must be engaged? And finally,

# LEADER

## *Position Overview*

Accountable for structuring, operating and perfecting the multiple communities of effort associated with the assigned SCOPE. Includes maintaining alignment with broader organizational and peer communities of effort and their corresponding strategies, cultures, objectives, purposes, and ecosystems (SCOPEs).

## *Functional Responsibilities*

1. Determining the ecosystem of relevant customers, collaborators and competitors as well as their primary interactions

2. Defining (and evolving as necessary) the purpose of all active communities of effort

3. Setting, sharing and pursuing long-term (visionary) and short-term objectives that contribute toward organizational objectives

4. Setting, sharing and pursuing cultural objectives as well as considering the impact of the culture on emerging strategies

5. Developing and deploying strategies that inform the resource deployment and actions required to meet all business and cultural objectives

6. Devising and deploying work methods (and technologies) aligned to the corresponding strategies, culture, objectives, purpose and ecosystem

7. Establishing and maintaining effective organizational structures that identify the roles, responsibilities, classification, number, location, title, and reporting relationship of the people required to pursue the designated objectives, strategies, and work methods

8. Acting to ensure all rewards and recognition systems are capable of attracting and retaining the required talent as well as incentivizing the right behaviors

9. Identifying, developing and securing the knowledge and capabilities needed to staff all communities of effort

10. Managing the tactical and financial planning processes that translate objectives and strategies into sequenced action (operational plans) and financial projections (budgets)

11. Achieving accountability by consistently and appropriately managing the assignment, execution, monitoring and evaluation of work, including taking consistent action to remediate substandard performance

12. Establishing and maintaining trusting relationships through consistent stakeholder engagement, including, but not limited to, employees, peers, superiors, suppliers, internal and external customers and relevant competitors

13. Pursuing individual, team and organizational development by exploring feedback and other data and clarifying plans of action

14. Coaching team members in the process of transforming and mastering new, more effective paradigms and procedures

it must be continuously *perfected*. Yesterday's excellence is today's standard and tomorrow's failure. In my mind, this makes for an extremely tangible framework for defining the work of a leader. Do you agree? Could you develop the job description using these three domains as your work functions?"

"Definitely. Seriously, Lake, my brain is exploding! This is a *very* useful model. I can see where mine might not have been wrong, exactly, but it wasn't helpful in explaining the core elements of the actual job—and it certainly is a job. Structure, operate, perfect. Structure, operate, perfect. I have to program this into my brain."

"I use the acronym 'SOP' as a mnemonic device. **Leadership-SOPs** is the name I've given to the framework and methodology."

"Oh, that works. I love the sound of it, but, actually, I usually think of SOPs as standard operating procedures."

"Well, yes, exactly!" Lake said with a huge smile. Franky looked at him a bit perplexed, not understanding the connection he was making. "**LeadershipSOPs** are your standard operating procedures for structuring, operating, and perfecting your communities of effort." He paused for effect—and to take a drink. "Essentially, it's a double entendre. I use the 'S,' 'O' and 'P' twice—first to describe my methodology, which involves the development of repeatable leadership processes, then another time to describe the framework which describes what the processes should do."

"Wow, I wished we had started here. I'm getting short on time . . . but my mind is racing in a thousand different directions!" Franky said, finally starting to feel like she knew how to tackle her challenge with Raj.

"Let's do this. I would like to spend our remaining minutes reflecting on the ideas we *explored* together, *clarifying* the insights they brought, and your next steps as they relate to our journey *and* the journey you intend to take with Raj."

"Yeah, yeah, yeah, I get it. **ECT(M)**. We'll restate the E and the C together, then I'll go after the T—which is

'Transform'—until we get it right and then, wham, we kick it into 'Master,'" Franky said, underlining the **ECT(M)** model in her notes.

"Ha, yes, that's exactly it."

"Sounds good. I wrote down the biggies as we were going along so that part should only take a minute or two. Then, we can focus on next steps. First, I haven't been 'all-in' in my partnership with Raj. This really blocked my best thinking, leading to a glaring mismatch between my assessment of his capabilities and the support I provided. Essentially, I set myself up for failure. Second, I need an actionable definition of leadership to help Raj. He doesn't understand the work of leading and I need to help him lead before focusing on helping him to lead well. The last thing I wrote and then underlined was, '**LeadershipSOPs** are your standard operating procedures for structuring, operating, and perfecting your communities of effort.' Truthfully, I am still unpacking that last one. It's only one sentence but there's a lot to chew on in there."

"Don't worry, I'm going to send over some reading materials for you to look over. In the meantime, let's just pull the string on it a little bit together. I'm sure you have a lot of informal **Leadership-SOPs** already. What's a good example of a leadership practice you repeat on a daily, weekly, monthly or even yearly basis? Or maybe one you only use when certain conditions present themselves?"

Franky thought for a moment. "I try to meet with every direct report for an hour once a month to talk about the more strategic items versus the transactional stuff we hit while bouncing from meeting to meeting."

"Perfect example."

"But then when you said yearly, my mind jumped to my strategic planning process. I don't quite do it yearly. More like every two years."

"Great, this is what I mean by **LeadershipSOPs**. I'd put the monthly one-on-ones under Operate, unless you're dedicating the time to coaching. Then I'd call that Perfect. As for strategic planning, I'd consider this as being under Structure since strategy is a key component of the basic architecture a community of effort, along with mission, vision, and all that stuff. My guess is you also have a routine way in which you communicate these processes to new team members, support staff, etcetera."

"Funny you should say that. An assistant of mine documented most of the major ones years ago. She titled it *The Care and Feeding of Franky* as a joke. My subsequent assistants have kept it up-to-date to make sure all this stuff makes it onto my calendar."

"Amazing! I love it. Let me ask you this. What do you think Raj's **LeadershipSOPs** look like?"

Franky's eyes went wide with excitement. Then, suddenly she realized what she was doing and why. "I have to go."

"Franky, maybe we could—"

"Can't wait for the next discussion, coach. I'm really excited. Honestly, I am. But I will explode if I don't get into action right now—and I mean, right now."

"Perhaps we could just—"

But Franky was already halfway across the room. There was no stopping her. "I'll send you an email with some files and my thoughts. Please read it before you . . ." The conference room door swung shut as Franky rushed out.

|  |  |  |  |

Franky felt bad about leaving like that. It was almost childish. She looked at herself in the rearview mirror and chuckled. Her mind was swimming. She began planning her discussion with Raj. Up until now, she felt completely helpless. But this idea was so simple. She was swelling with confidence. Only one thing stood in her way and that is what she was on a mission to hit head-on.

She looked at her actual speed. *Perhaps 25 miles per hour over the speed limit is a touch too fast.* Speaking of speed, she started think about what Lake had said. *I have to mirror my process with him when*

*I engage Raj. I need to slow things down. I can't just rush in and tell him what do. Raj has to choose to work with me and I have to let him talk. I need to better understand what's going on in his mind. Above all, I must get him to accept my partnership and then—*

She slammed on the gas. *Okay, maybe a little speeding wouldn't hurt.*

# CHAPTER EIGHT

# THE

# EXECUTIVE

Raj was more than just a little alarmed when Franky barged into the lab. She looked uncharacteristically disheveled. Several different scenarios flashed across his mind as they walked back to his office together—none of them anything less than horrid.

"Thanks Raj, I only need a few minutes and then you can get back to it." Franky said as she scooted down the hall.

*She sounds more anxious than I am. Oh no, she's resigning! That's even worse than staying!*

"Franky, is everything okay?"

"Not yet, but I hope it will be.

"My goodness, what has happened?"

"Let me start again. I didn't mean to scare you. Nothing's happened. Not really. Well, something but nothing you need to worry about. It's a good thing, I suppose."

"Franky, I don't—"

She cut him off midsentence, "I'm sorry. Very, very sorry."

"For what? I don't understand what you're saying—"

Franky cut him off again. "Please don't be angry, Raj. I mean I'm sorry. That's why I am here to say—to apologize to you."

"But what on earth for?" asked Raj, feeling much more irritated now than anxious.

Franky began to laugh, "Well, right now, I'm sorry for botching this apology. Perhaps Lake was right."

"Lake? The coach? What does he have to do with this? Did he tell you to do this?"

"No, no he didn't." She said, laughing. "In fact, he told me . . . how did he say it? 'Don't just do something; sit there.'"

"Perhaps he was right." Raj signaled to Franky to take a seat.

Sitting, Franky straightened her suit jacket, then looked quizzically at him. "Raj? Was that . . . intentional? Was that a joke?" She said as if doubting he were capable of such a thing.

"Franky, you have an interesting way of apologizing. You burst into my lab, drag me down here, then insult my sense of humor?" Raj widened his eyes to emphasize his amazement."

"Oh dear." Franky hung her head.

"Ah ha, I am joking! You see. Ha! Sarcasm. You see? I am not the mad scientist everyone makes me out to be."

A huge smile spread across Raj's face. Franky burst into laughter and he actually joined her. She seemed to collect herself in the silence that followed. "Thank you, Raj, I needed that. Let me start over . . . again. I'm coming directly from my first meeting with Lake. In fact, I didn't even finish the meeting." Franky paused. "It was very enlightening."

"That sounds more like an argument for staying rather than leaving early."

"Very true! But I couldn't stay another minute without having this conversation." She paused again. "Raj, I botched things between us. I didn't know how badly until Lake called me on it."

"Well, I certainly didn't like how you got here, if that's what you mean, but things have improved in the last several months. I will not deny that."

"Thank you, but please let me finish. It turns out that while your respect for me was perhaps rising, I was less and less deserving of it. I wanted to help the team but I—I didn't try hard enough to help *you*. I saw you struggling and let it confirm my opinion that you were beyond help."

"Franky, your apologies are somewhat insulting." Raj said, trying not to react too poorly to her strange, meandering words.

"Don't you see? I told you I wanted your trust and your partnership, but I didn't extend any. In fact, I acted from the start as if *you* were the problem and I needed to work around you, instead of with you." Franky sighed. "My job as your partner and the CEO is to support you. Raj, this company is lucky to have you. The entire world is lucky to have you . . . and someday soon it's going to know it! And I should have asked you this before going around your back, but I was too stupid, and I suppose too scared to do it." Franky's voice changed a bit. "Raj, will you *allow* me to be the CEO of this . . . of *your* company?"

"Um, you already have the job. Like I said before, I'm as stuck with you as you are with me."

"That's the problem though, isn't it? We can't just be two people who are stuck with each other. We must buy into this partnership at a deeper level."

"No offense, Franky, but I don't know if I can give you that. I don't hate you or anything. I even appreciate you at times. But that's all I have in me."

"I understand and I'm not even here to ask you for anything, I guess. I shouldn't have even implied that I was looking for . . ." She began again. "My focus is on me and my false start—what I did wrong. I'm here to apologize for not already giving you the respect and partnership you deserved. I can and will do better. I believe in your vision and I believe in you. You are not beyond help. You are not alone. And I'm honored to be at the table. I came reluctantly and then when I did, I botched things. When I needed your trust and partnership the most, I let you down. Now please, I've pulled you away for long enough. That's all I needed to say. Thank you for your time. Thanks for listening."

*We broke her. She's lost her mind.* Raj thought as Franky exited without another word.

| | | | |

It was well after 11 p.m. Raj sat in his office, reviewing the data for a fourth time. He had been running and rerunning the same data for days. *Could this be right?* His hands trembled, but not with the excitement you might expect from someone whose data showed his treatment regime was essentially ready for Phase II of the clinical trials. No, the feeling Raj slowly became aware of was something else.

*Why am I so uneasy? I feel like I am going to be sick.*

His mind kept returning to the odd discussion with Franky a few weeks before. He hated to admit it, but there was something enjoyable about seeing that side of her. He had never thought of her as vulnerable before. She was normally stitched together so tightly he didn't even think of her as having emotions. *It felt good to hear her say those things—and not just because they were so hard for her to get out. She meant what she said, and she was right to say them. But why didn't I thank her? Why didn't I tell her right then and there that I would partner with her? I clearly need her.*

But, as soon as he articulated the question, he knew why. It would have been a betrayal. *I started this journey with Mak. She doesn't get to stab me in the back, then just step into his shoes and replace him. It isn't fair.*

Raj leaned back in his chair, strangling the armrests. The anger he felt was better than the fear suffocating him a moment before. And so he fed it. *How dare she—how could she manipulate Lily . . . hiding behind concern for the team . . . concern for her money, more like it.*

After a moment, Raj loosened his grip on the chair as his anger started to betray him, as anger often does, and turn inward. *The company was mine to rescue or ruin. It wasn't my fault, though. I had to get the science right. What choice did I have? I should have reached out. I chose not to. It was too hard. Why do I always do that? I just dug a hole and hid.*

Raj rested his elbows on his desk, cradling his head in his hands. He closed his tired eyes and rubbed them. Deciding to give his eyes a break, he pinched the bridge of his nose to relieve pressure from his relentless headache.

He sat in silence. Even the janitorial staff was long gone. His anger melted into disappointment, then hardened back into fear. *Who am I without this puzzle to solve? Do I know what comes next?* He suddenly realized he didn't know the first thing about actually delivering a drug to market or being chief scientific officer, not really. He was a research scientist, perhaps one of the best, but he didn't know the first thing about running a department, let alone a company. His breathing hastened and then suddenly stopped altogether.

*Oh no! Am I having a heart attack? What's wrong with me? Why can't I breathe!* His body convulsed as he tried to suck in some air. *Breathe damn it. Breathe!*

The crippling silence finally ended as Raj won his battle with his body, taking in an enormous breath. For a moment, he felt relief. Then, he started to sob. Tears streamed down his face. Raj hadn't let himself cry a single tear for his mother or his friend . . . or himself. Instead, he bottled it up inside, using the pressure to power his work. But something had broken loose inside him. He was afraid to let it out, but he couldn't hold it in any longer.

As the sobs subsided, Raj felt embarrassed and confused by his outburst. He sat quietly for several minutes. Then he swiveled his chair to face his computer screen. He typed out two sentences and hit send before even adding a subject:

Still looking for a job? As it happens, I need a CEO . . . and a partner.

*See Franky, I am funny.*

| | | | |

Raj didn't quite regret his late-night email, but he wasn't exactly comfortable with it either. He was even less comfortable when he saw Franky arrive and walk toward his office. At least at this time of morning, there weren't any witnesses to compound his shame.

"Good morning. Nice to see you up here for a change," Franky said kindly, popping her head around the doorjamb.

"Good morning. Did you, uh . . . get my . . ."

"I certainly did. I was pleased to hear from you and it just so happens I am in the market for a new opportunity. I kind of screwed up my old one." She smiled. "Our beginnings don't have to define our endings, do they? We can choose each other this time and make a go of it as partners, right?"

Raj's stomach churned as he struggled to find courage to say the words he had rehearsed all night. "Franky, the big problems are essentially solved . . . from a scientific perspective, I mean. We're ready to enter Phase II. The results are in. We have definitively confirmed the treatment is safe at the target dose. There are, of course, a number of details to iron out with the FDA. But *we* are ready."

"Seriously? That's fantastic!"

"No, it's not." Raj paused, still searching for strength. "I'm terrified of what's next. I don't really know anything about the way forward from here. Every step is into the unknown. And I've driven most of the real talent away. Steve is barely speaking to me and he's not the only one."

"Raj, we can't get the last year back. But we can be different today. Besides, the good news is, it takes more effort to get the rock rolling than to keep it going."

"I feel like that makes me the rock." Raj tried to be funny but could hardly muster the energy.

"No, it makes us two tired souls looking for a lever long enough and a place to stand."

"'. . . a fulcrum on which to place it,' I believe."

"What?"

"Archimedes said . . ."

"Raj," Franky said playfully.

"Yes?"

"Stick to biochemistry. No need to best me in all the sciences, partner."

| | | | |

Raj tapped on the glass wall of Franky's office. "Is this time still good?"

Franky looked over her shoulder. "Absolutely. Take a seat. I'm just finishing up an email. *And* send. I'm done. Are you ready for this?" She swiveled her chair away from her computer, rolling it behind her desk.

"I am not sure quite what to expect, but know I need to do something differently."

"Well, let me start by setting some expectations and ground rules."

"We need ground rules? Sounds like overkill," Raj said nervously.

"We'll determine them together. It'll take two seconds. I just want to separate the kinds of discussions we'll be having during these meetings from our other, more business-focused chats."

"I don't understand. I thought we were going to talk about my—*our* challenges."

"You see. There you go. This is why I wanted to start with expectations." Franky paused, before beginning again. "I want to use this time to do something deeper than just talking about challenges. I want to explore the heart of the matter first and build from there. Would you do that with me?"

"Can't we just focus on all of the work that has to get done? I'm worried sitting around 'exploring' might not be the best use of our time given . . . given the magnitude of what's occurring and all the time I've wasted."

Franky smiled, "Boy, Raj, we're more alike than you know. I said almost the same thing to Lake during my first coaching session."

"You mean, the one you liked so much you left early?" Raj joked, relaxing a bit at the thought of how this process had affected Franky.

She laughed with him. "Exactly, I didn't want to do it, either, but it was enlightening. Besides, we got down to business soon enough. Like you, I was feeling all this pressure to act—but it turned out the anxiety alarm bells I was hearing weren't demanding action. They were begging for reflection. I can't promise you the same outcome, but I would like to guide you on a similar journey . . . if you're willing."

Raj sighed, "It sounds like the sort of thing I would never do, which is perhaps the best sign I should." Raj took a deep breath, let it back out and smiled. "Let's do it."

"Great, the process Lake taught me starts with exploration, moves to clarifying action and then taking action to transform your leadership behaviors. After that, provided your behavior *experiments* work out, you'll set out on the path to mastery. Like I said, even though I fought it at first, I found it very helpful in getting me to uncover some important stuff I was ignoring or in some cases resisting. I was beginning to feel like our situation was hopeless, but this process helped me move past these classic stages of dealing with such unwanted change and re-engage."

"I think this is true for me, too. I am embarrassed to say this, but I don't think I properly mourned the death of my mother, let alone Mak's. It sounds silly, but I think it's behind a lot of my . . . my behavior."

"Well, that's just it, Raj, people deal with transformation and change a lot like they deal with death . . . which is to say, not well. The whole purpose of starting with exploration is to: make sure we aren't ignoring any important data; lower your resistance to making real changes; and overcome the natural feelings of

# GETTING INTO ACTION

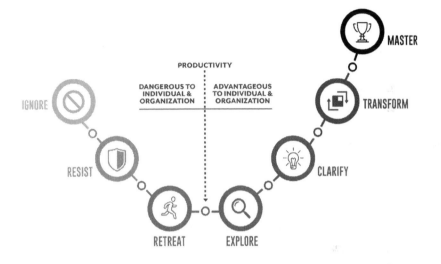

The **ECT(M)** Transformation Model is designed
specifically to help people, teams, and organizations overcome
the negative (but normal) impacts of change.

helplessness associated with all this grief. Both of us responded normally, we just hung onto it way too long. This is our chance to let go of it and move forward . . . together."

"Make sense?"

"Too much . . ."

"So, onto ground rules then. I would like to ask you for a level of candor that is difficult between any two people, let alone ones with our history. In return, I will not share the information you provide regarding your internal thoughts or feelings with anyone."

"Or . . .?"

"Or, I will have violated these ground rules and your trust, thereby condemning us both to failure."

Raj smirked. "Okay, I'll do my best to trust you. Trust is hard for me, though. Not so much candor. Candor is where I usually go wrong."

"Fair enough. In return, I'll do my best not to react negatively to what you're saying. I will assume you are sharing what's going through your mind to help us move forward, not derail us. Are there any ground rules you would like to add?"

Raj sat in silence for a minute, taking Franky's question seriously. "You will need to push me and sometimes push back on me. I can be quite stubborn when I'm trying to incorporate new information into what I think I already know. My wife says I apply the same level of confidence I have in biochemistry to areas I actually know very little about."

"You don't say." Franky shot Raj a tight-lipped but friendly grin.

"So, I guess I would like to be pushed, a little, and, of course, the candor and confidentiality piece goes both ways."

"Excellent. Let's get started then before we both jump out of our seats." Franky opened her folio. "As I've been working with Lake, I have been writing down things I think will help us." She paged through at least 20 pages of notes, explaining to Raj that she and Lake had been busy for the past few weeks. When she found what she was looking for, she looked up. "Let's start with your job. How would you define it?"

Raj felt confused by the elementary nature of her question but decided to play along. "Well, you know my job. I'm the chief scientific officer." Franky signaled for Raj to keep going. "I'm the head biochemical expert for Techular Biologics and the executive in charge of research, lab operations, and clinical trials."

"Interesting."

"What is?"

"That you listed expert *before* executive. Why do you think that is? Was it a conscious choice or just happenstance?"

"I suppose it's the part of the job I identify with most. The part I understand." He sighed heavily, then mumbled, "The part I'm actually doing."

Franky leaned forward with a bit of a smirk settling on her face. "There you go. I couldn't have said it better myself. You nailed it."

"Nailed what? We both already know—"

Franky interrupted him, "From expert to executive. That's your development objective! What do you think about that?"

"It's terrifying." Raj said jovially.

"Well, let's demystify it together. We'll take its power away."

"How do we do that?"

"We'll work together to create your new job description; one that focuses on being an executive rather than an expert."

"But my team isn't even capable of—"

"Why not?" Franky cut him off again, anticipating where he was going.

Raj realized they were back to question and answer mode again. He decided to reflect on his answer this time before blurting something out. "I've lost all the really experienced scientists I brought in, even my second-in-command."

"And why is that?"

"Because, they didn't like how I did things. They were constantly second-guessing me or running off in the wrong direction."

"I thought these were your most experienced scientists."

"They were. It's not as if our disagreements were substantive scientific disagreements, just procedural choices that vary from researcher to researcher, just preferences." Raj explained with a bit of edge to his voice. He could feel himself getting more defensive with each question.

"I see. And what about their straying from the priority work? What was that about? Did you clarify the priorities? Did they know where you needed them."

Franky's questions were really starting to frustrate him. They didn't seem that helpful after all. "What do you mean? Of course, I told them."

"Easy, we're just trying to get to the bottom of this together. I wasn't there so I need to know what you know to help."

Raj's tone didn't change but his aim did. This time he snapped inward, scolding himself for bad behavior. "Look, I did communicate the priorities but in a way no one would like, particularly not scientists of their caliber. And the truth is, I didn't need them to do what I was doing. I just wasn't able to direct their efforts across a whole new path while completing my own research. It was just too much for me to oversee all at once."

"I see. So, you think they left because there really wasn't room for them in your model?"

"I suppose you could say that. I wanted them on the team. I needed their expertise. But I really wasn't prepared to just set them loose in the lab."

"Can I offer some observations?"

"That's why I am here." He said while rubbing his face. "Sorry, that didn't come out right."

"No worries. We started down this path because I proposed we do a role reset. You wisely objected because you know if you fill a new role, there will be a huge gap your team can't fill."

"Correct," He said flatly.

"Well, I'm thinking that may be a good thing."

"I'm not sure I take your meaning. How could that be a good thing?"

"Well, I don't know a lot about the dynamics in your lab. But I have seen a pattern over the years with leaders who *do* too much. Try to picture this visual. When they lean into the team's . . ." Franky stood up, leaning way over the desk. She physically moved her head toward Raj's. Raj instinctively withdrew a few inches to preserve his personal space. "Exactly . . . everyone else leans out. Because if they didn't, they would smack heads with their boss. It seems like you saw both behaviors. You had some actual head-butts—not over important issues, just the kind of stuff people prefer to keep their own counsel on. Then you also had some people leaning out and trying to find other work to do—a different way or place to add value. Presumably, work they could do without their boss looking over their shoulder."

"I see what you're saying but they were new and I was right in the middle of the biggest breakthrough of my career."

"Raj, I truthfully can't say whether or not you had a choice then. You were doing something no one else had ever tried. But that is a dead argument with very little relevance at present. The *real* question is, how will you do it this time? Could you build a new operating model for your departments with a new role for you and substantial roles for experienced scientists?"

"We definitely can. It's just the transition will be difficult. I mean, we are about to hit a whole new phase of complexity. It's going to require skills nobody has. Not even me!" Raj could feel his anxiety rising again.

"It sounds like the perfect time."

"What? I don't think you're listening. I'm worried I don't have the skills for what comes next, let alone my department." The edge was back to his voice.

"It sounds like, if anything, that might make it easier for you to stay out of work that isn't yours anyway. I think you are making a great case for some new roles. How many and at what level? Who will they work with most? Who will they report to?" Franky said, sounding like she actually enjoyed this stuff.

*This isn't going to work. I can't do this. I hate everything about it.*

Raj exhaled loudly, trying to keep his emotions in check. "I'm having trouble articulating myself. You're right. But I'm just . . . it feels like I . . . I know science. I do not know how to do any of this! I've never been good with people. I have no patience for them. I have difficulty trusting them. They exhaust me. They want things I can't possibly give . . . things I don't even *want* to give."

"So, you think leadership is about the work or the people?"

"Both, I guess. It's about getting people to do the work."

"Hmm, I not sure I fully agree. But let's use your definition for a minute for argument's sake."

"Well, I'm not sure it's *the* definition. I was just trying to answer your question."

"Fair enough. My point is, even by your own thinking, there is an overwhelming focus on understanding, motivating, and guiding people."

"Yes, this is true. Of course, it's true. It's also my point."

"Well, to be honest—and here comes that candor you asked for—what troubles me is you seem to have no interest in tending to these things. When we talk about the people, I can hear your frustration."

"Are you trying to talk me out of my job? Is that what this is about?" Raj blurted out in an irritated panic.

"No, I'm sorry if that came out wrong. But I think we have stumbled upon the most important thing we could be discussing."

"Really?" Raj said, his temperature rising. "Which is what?"

"Do you want to be a leader?" Franky asked gently.

"That's not the first time you've asked me that question and frankly it's insulting!" Raj blurted out.

"You're right. It's a terrible question. Let me ask another one. *Why* do you want to be a leader?"

"What do you even mean? Because this is my company. My vision! Mak and I started it together. None of this would even exist without my work."

"Let me try this again. Every word you said is true. Yet, none spoke to why you want to be a leader," said Franky.

Raj's anger got away from him, "I thought you were going to help me. This doesn't feel like help. It feels like sabotage." Raj slammed his hands on the desk. "You want me to step aside from this job too! You want me out of the way. What possible use could I be now that the real science is done?"

Franky blinked slowly. Raj read disappointment in her face. "Raj," she said softly. "I can see I pushed too hard. Do you honestly believe I'm trying to push you out instead of help?"

"I don't know what to believe. I'm just very frustrated. And now, now, I am . . . confused."

"I was just applying the same logic to your leadership decision as we applied to our relationship. If you don't enter into this leadership thing willingly, every struggle becomes an unwanted entanglement, something to resent instead of figure out. Imagine if you had lacked the vision and dedication to press on against the odds for all these years. Something in you loved the challenge. Something in you found it very satisfying to unravel layer after layer in your search for a solution. And, I'd venture to guess something in you is already missing it, wondering who you really are without it. I guess I am suggesting unravelling organizational entanglements and solving people puzzles could be your new area of study, your new challenge. But if you don't want it, if you aren't able to come to the table with a willingness to struggle through it and get it wrong every day until you get it right, you'll never survive the journey."

Raj was still standing. As the adrenaline washed out of his muscles, he experienced a massive emotional drain. Franky's words had hit the mark too well, but he didn't know how to answer. He didn't know what to say or do. *I don't know if I can do this.* He felt sick. He started moving toward the door. He needed to escape. It was all he could do to mumble, "I have to go."

|||||

Raj fell asleep the instant his head hit the pillow, possibly before. He was spent. It had probably been six or seven years since he went to bed this early.

At 3:34 a.m., he woke as suddenly as he had fallen asleep. His mind was clear. He grabbed for his phone, almost knocking it off his nightstand. After managing to close his fingers around it, he brought to his face, clumsily opening his email. He thumbed a single sentence with no subject:

"I can't ignore my duty to lead the people who have come to answer our cries for help."

He laid the phone down on his chest, breathing deeply in and out. He felt uncharacteristically relaxed. Grounded. For the first time since starting Techular, he felt a responsibility to engage with the large community of people around him. He had no idea how to move forward from here, but at least for the moment, it didn't matter.

His phone vibrated just as he was drifting back to sleep. He smiled to himself. Without looking, he knew it was Franky.

|||||

The next time Raj opened his eyes, it was 6:05 a.m. He skimmed over his messages, clicking on Franky's reply. It read:

"Excellent. My office: 7a.m.?"

The calm that had washed over Raj was replaced with nervous energy. He quickly typed out a response, buying himself some extra minutes. It was going to be a challenge getting to the office in time. Orange County's traffic wasn't anything like Los Angeles's, but it was no picnic, either. He rushed through his morning routine, surprised to find the traffic cooperating.

When he arrived, Franky was in her office waiting for him.

"Good morning," she said. "I grabbed us coffee since you said you were running behind and it was a late night for both of us."

"I do need some help waking up. But, believe it or not, I slept better and longer last night than since I can remember. Our discussion wiped me out. Then, I woke up in the middle of the night and it was all so clear."

"Ha. I'm so glad to hear it. It had the opposite effect on me. I was lying awake half the night."

"I'm sorry. I know I left abruptly. And I'm sure my email at three in the morning made it even worse."

"Are you serious? It was the highlight of my night!" She said, making Raj laugh. "No, seriously, I was sure I had set us back by being too pushy."

"Ugh, I am like a teenager who has been cooped up in the house playing too many video games. I have been closed off from the world, from even myself for a long time. It is going to take some pushing to get me to go outside and play with the other kids. Maybe even some dynamite," Raj smiled.

"Well, if it makes you feel better, I was on an emotional rollercoaster during my first coaching session with Lake. I was fighting with him one minute, apologizing the next. And, as you know, I didn't stick around for the end either." They both laughed. "In retrospect, I guess I should have expected your early departure. And speaking of Lake, we've been exploring his leadership framework and methodology in our sessions. I'm surprised at how practical and helpful his model is. In fact, I'd eventually like to introduce it to the whole team. But I thought maybe I could start with just you and me first—to see how it works for us."

"Yes, better to start off with the hardest nut to crack."

"Oh Raj, we have plenty of nuts here to go around." Franky quipped back. "Seriously though, it'll be helpful to us since it puts the focus on the real work of leading, not an endless list of interpersonal skills and leadership styles."

"You had me back at practical." Raj said before taking a long pull on his coffee. *Wow, this coffee is good.* Raj pulled the cup away from his mouth to check the label. He was surprised to find it was from his regular stop down the street.

"Do you cook?" Franky asked.

Raj almost spit out the coffee. "Um. No. Why?"

"Good," Franky said, sounding pleased with herself.

"You aren't the first person to say that." Raj said playfully.

"What I mean is I have been trying to think of an analogy that works for both of us. I had a hunch cooking might be a good one. Because, as my husband will tell you, even boiling water is outside my comfort zone."

"Who knew we had so much in common?"

"If you and I were to suddenly decide it was important to learn to cook, what do you think we'd need to do—other than up our fire insurance policies?"

"I guess we'd need to decide what we wanted to cook, get a recipe or watch a video, then give it a try." Raj answered.

"Perfect. This analogy is going to work great. I was thinking about it in much the same way. We'd need to know what to cook, get or create a recipe, buy the ingredients, then try it a few times until we liked the results. Now, if we apply this line of thinking to leading, we could say we need to establish what leading is to understand what we're trying to do and get the right ingredients to make the dish. Next, we would need to look up, beg, borrow, or steal the recipes on how to mix our ingredients together. Then finally, we'd start cooking until we get it right, adding in the extra techniques as we discover or develop them over time."

"Okay, I follow you. It makes sense, but I don't think I learned how to lead in the process. Was I supposed to?"

"No, just the method. Recipes! We need to know what we are making and then create the recipes. When I tried to help you before, I didn't bother with giving you the whole recipe or even tell you what you were making. All I did was yell down the hall, 'needs more salt!'"

Raj's face lit up. "Yes! Now I see what you are saying. I didn't have a recipe . . . and you didn't give me one. And, to be honest, you didn't tell me how much to add, when to add it, or even why."

"Exactly. We need to explore what meals you need to make, meaning we need to determine your work versus the teams' work, acquire the ingredients, or the people and resources, engage them with the right recipes, and just get better and better at it as we go."

"I like it," said Raj with genuine excitement.

"Lake calls this approach **LeadershipSOPs**."

"Sure, Standard Operating Procedures for leading. Makes sense."

"Exactly, except there is a bonus meaning hidden in there. He uses each letter in the S.O.P. acronym twice . . . so it stands for your *standard operating procedures for structuring, operating, and perfecting* your community of effort."

"Structuring, operating, and perfecting."

"Yes, it fits with what we were saying before. As a leader, you must develop and deploy recipes to *structure* your team, meaning the process by which you determine the strategy, the work, and the organization. Likewise, once you've established your structure, you need to establish routines to *operate* or engage it, like planning out the tactics, assigning the work and holding people accountable, engaging stakeholders, stuff like that. And then, finally, you also need to determine how to *perfect* the team, meaning your systems for developing the people and improving the results."

# RECIPE

## PREP WORK

1. Gather and prioritize topics
2. Create agenda
3. Assign topics to team members
4. Provide direction on expectations regarding length and process
5. Collate all slides
6. Send invitations to visitors

## EQUIPMENT

1. Conf. room
2. Large monitor
3. Video conf. eq.
4. 2 laptops
5. 1 HDMI cable

## BI-WEEKLY MANAGEMENT TEAM MEETING

### INGREDIENTS

1. Me
2. All direct reports (including individual contributors)
3. All leaders reporting to my direct reports
4. Visitors as determined by prep work

### DIRECTIONS

1. Open virtual meeting rooms and project title slide 10 minutes before start
2. Assemble physically available members in time fora prompt start
3. Begin with an enterprise update and emergent issues roundtable (critical items only)
4. Assign one member of the team to capture action items via laptop for speedy distribution
5. Facilitate for 2 hours (or until all topics are covered)
6. Use final 30 minutes to recap action items and add informational updates
7. End by highlighting the efforts of at least one team member or function

"It all sounds so simple."

"My husband tells me the same thing about cooking! Of course, I don't want to cook, so it all remains a convenient mystery to me. The point is to demystify leading and get you into action. I like the concept because most of the leadership training I'm familiar with focuses on the soft skills that help you do things better without clarifying the hard skills and hard work of the job. Doing it like this gets you leading first, which means you're practicing and improving as you go."

"Definitely, let's get started on my structure then," Raj said, showing his excitement to charge right in. "We could probably knock that out this week."

"Your structure is a great place to start, particularly since we have established immediate needs in that area. However, we need to keep in mind that you already have a team, or as Lake would call it, 'a community of effort.'"

"I don't know what the difference between team and 'community of effort' is, but I'm not sure why having one is a barrier to starting with my structure. Didn't you say we need to get that right first? Won't it help to get this straightened out . . . or at least give us a sense for where we're going?"

"Yes, absolutely, I think *structure* should be a priority and we should talk about it during our coaching sessions. But what I mean is, I don't think we should do the actual work in this room—with just to two of us."

"I don't follow." Raj said, genuinely perplexed.

"We can discuss the how, who, when, and why together. And then you can use the recipes to engage your team, build buy-in, ownership, and alignment."

"I get it. We'll build the recipes, the **LeadershipSOPs** together, then I can use them to engage and improve my team. So, are we kind of doing all three: structure, operate, and perfect all at once?"

"In a way. As we dig into each area, you will find that as distinct as each domain is, they are also completely interconnected. Speaking of interconnected, you asked about the term, *community of effort*. You are right that you can think of it as synonymous with a team, department, or even an entire organization."

"Why not just say that then?" Raj asked a little sharply, feeling frustrated at the introduction of complexity when simplicity would suffice.

"I think you can and should if it's more helpful. In all my work with Lake, he has never suggested we should take his framework and methodology verbatim. His focus is on leaders establishing a definition for leading which informs comprehensive, consistent, and effective action with a bent toward continuous improvement. That said, I'm personally using it because it seems to fit so well with what I already knew but wasn't articulating clearly. Anyhow, that's a long-winded way of saying, don't use it if you don't like it. But before you make your decision, let me tell you why I like it."

"Fair enough." Raj said with a little skepticism in his voice.

"Well, I suppose what *community of effort* has over the more common term, *team*, is how descriptive it is. The word team is so ubiquitous, it has almost lost its bite. Community of effort implies a group of people who are united by their willingness and ability to act interdependently." Franky paused for Raj to reply, but he motioned for her to continue. "For me, I like the *effort* part the best . . . because I always thought of leadership as very goal-centric. But that is problematic if you think about it."

"Sounds practical to me," Raj said.

"Only on the surface. If you think about it though, it sets you up for an 'ends justifies the means' situation, in which it's the work and the goal, not the people and their collective capabilities that matter. Think about it this way. Your need for this whole organization arose because you had an objective you couldn't achieve alone. To realize this goal, you needed the *means* to achieve it. So, the purpose of leading, for you finding and engaging all these people is to build the means to achieve your goal. Do you see what I'm saying? It's slippery but important. If you mistake your ultimate goal for your priority focus, it messes up your ability to generate the means to achieve it. You end up mistaking the team's work for your work. Essentially, leadership is the process we use to cultivate a community of effort. If you could do it alone, you wouldn't need to lead."

Raj was deep in thought so Franky continued, "Think about it this way: achieving a goal isn't adequate proof that you led. Similarly, failing to achieve a goal does not mean you failed to lead. Whereas, if you engage a group of people in a way that creates a willing and capable community of effort, you most definitely are leading, regardless of goal-achievement. Does that make sense? Your primary goal as a leader is assembling a high-performance engine, not winning the race. Winning the race is the team's primary objective and your secondary objective—otherwise you give away the *means* in pursuit of the *ends*."

Raj brought his hands to his face, laughing quietly. He took a deep breath before speaking. "Oh Franky," he said in a soft voice.

"Still not buying it? Worried about where accountability fits in? I think that was my best shot."

"Yes, yes, I'm buying it. What you're saying just hit me like a ton of bricks. You are describing exactly what I have done. I gave away my 'means,' my community of effort, in favor of what I saw as the more important 'ends' and now I have no 'means' left to move forward. This is probably the most important part. At least for me . . . and my instinct was to toss it to the curb as just extra words. Creating a community of effort is the purpose of leading. My new job is to create communities of effort all over this company." Raj continued, repeating variations of the thought to himself. Then he blurted out, "Ugh, what is wrong with me? I do not hate people. I am not a bad person. This is just never going to be easy—or natural for me. My wires are crossed or something."

"Don't be so hard on yourself," Franky said supportively. "You don't need to change who you are. We are simply going to create **LeadershipSOPs** to trigger more effective *behaviors* so you don't have to rely on instinct alone. Instincts are reactive. **LeadershipSOPs** are strategic. Think of this methodology as a leadership lifehack. You're outsmarting your current instinctual habits by replacing them with new, more strategic **LeadershipSOPs**. Sure, it will feel funny at first because it's the opposite of what you have been doing. But over time, repetition will make it more comfortable, more routine and natural. At the same time, the repetition and the tiny improvements you'll naturally make each time will grow your skill and confidence as well as the team's. This is the same reason sports teams practice the same individual skills and team plays over and over again. It gives the leaders and the players the experience they need to trust each other and collaborate better and better."

Raj looked down deep in thought. *Can you over-write instincts with SOPs? Is that even possible?* He was feeling exhausted by himself. Then, he suddenly thought about the SOPs he had used in the lab for years and how they had become so ritualistic that he didn't even need to think about them anymore. He just did them. It actually felt weird *not* to do them. *When was the last time I forgot to use protective equipment or failed to log the results of an experiment?* He couldn't recall a single time. He started thinking of more and more SOPs he had built over the years. *Really, they define everything I do in the lab. They are the culmination of everything I know about actually performing the work.*

For the first time in a while, he experienced a strange feeling: genuine interest in a topic other than biochemistry.

*This stuff is kind of a science all of its own.*

# CHAPTER NINE

# THE
# APPLICANT

Sara Chen hated being judged by people. You never knew what secret prejudices they brought to the table, or if a bad mood might color their opinion. The same went with relationships. You might have a pleasant conversation with someone one day, and the next, this person might snap your head off, just because they didn't get enough sleep or had a fight with their significant other or . . . well, whatever.

People always had a thousand excuses for bad behavior. Maybe that's why Sara found such comfort in science, gravitating to the field as a young woman. She made a point of putting more into her science fair projects than other kids. While they (or more accurately, their parents) were busy creating lame baking soda volcanoes, she crafted intricate kinetic sculptures and fashioned color-changing solutions out of cabbage—all on her own. Her painstaking efforts and genuine talent took her all the way to first place every year, an honor that invariably prompted a pleased grunt from her dad, who seemed to speak mostly in grunts and groans.

*She lived for those grunts.* To both her and her brother, they were crumbs thrown to starving hearts. And they motivated them both to achieve. Facts and formulas brought her rewards that personal opinions couldn't dispute. And as she grew up, they became her reliable constants.

*Her high school and college peers?* Not so much. They would take her on unpredictable roller-coaster rides. She kept her smile in place, but built a wall around her as she latched onto science with laserlike intensity.

*Nine times out of 10, more people mean more contaminants. I don't just block them out as a preference; it's my job. My results must be free from outside influences. Clean and accurate results are what matter. People are messy. Ugh, not helpful—time to reframe!*

Today *had* to be about people, or at least *a* person. Today, she had to please a particular someone to get the job of her dreams—a leadership role at one of the most renowned biotech firms in the country. As she neared the address on Google Maps, she did the rhythmic breathing exercises her brother taught her to help lower her anxiety and boost her confidence.

*I can do this. I will do this. I have the experience, the expertise. This isn't just about my needs. It's about theirs. They need me. Yeah, that's right. Okay, maybe a little less cocky. Right . . . this is about the value I bring as an experienced and globally recognized researcher. Yes! That's how I will nail this interview. I will nail this interview. I will nail this . . .*

| | | | |

"Sara Chen. Very pleased to meet you," said the man behind a desk as he skimmed her resume. "Stanford. Summa cum laude." He looked up with an impressed smile. "Amazing track record at Endosystems Engineering."

Feeling her hands sweat, she wiped them on her linen slacks. *No way he saw me do that over his desk.* Nor, hopefully, could he sense the panic threatening to overwhelm her. She had expected to be talking to Evan, a lab manager at Techular. Instead, when she came into reception, she was floored to find herself ushered into this office—to a seat in front of this man. He was practically a legend. She glanced to her right, observing the business of the lab through the window.

*Why am I here? I am totally not prepared for this!*

As he continued scanning her credentials, she tried to calm her nerves by glancing around at his clean and well-organized office, gathering clues about what he was all about. Scientific journals, reference books, and lab logs filled tidy bookshelves. On the walls, she noticed pictures of him shaking hands with some of the greatest names in scientific circles today—the kind of company she expected he would keep.

*OMG, is that him receiving his Nobel Prize? Ugh! This isn't helping. Look him in the eyes. Look him in the eyes.*

The man smiled at her again. "By the way, I read your most recent research papers. Very promising. Excellent work. Well thought-out and detail-oriented, both elements I admire."

*Is Raj Patel actually complimenting me?* She stiffened, forcing an awkward smile.

"Well, it's nothing like what you've done. I mean, not yet—but I do think there are some applications we could examine here, together." *Too far . . .reel yourself back in!* "Sorry, didn't mean to be presumptuous. I-I'm just excited. Excited to be speaking to you. I didn't even think that I would, you know, get to interview with you directly."

"Please, relax. The only difference between us is time," laughed Raj.

"Your work, though. It's helped so many people."

"Yes, I am very humbled by what Techular has accomplished. My only regret is it wasn't ready in time to help my own mother."

"Oh, yes, I recall hearing that story. I am so sorry."

"Thank you, it was hard. I've had many challenges, but challenges, I've learned, if you face them, force you to grow. And that can be a good thing."

She nodded; afraid speaking might raise something else

problematic. She didn't want to wade into any more personal matters that might impact his mood.

"Sara," he said, taking an extra beat to fix his eyes on her. "I
want you to relax. I know you were expecting to meet with Evan,
our research manager. And he will be talking to you after we're
done. But I had to jump in front due to my schedule. I make it a
point to participate in the hiring process for all our leadership positions. Plus, I have to say, when he sent me your CV, I was intrigued.
And since I know Jamie Williams—"

"Oh, Jamie's great! I was sad when he left Endosystems. I didn't
get to work with him too much at my level, but enough to make a
real impact on me. It was an honor to get to learn from him."

"You're being too humble. He thinks you're great, too. As a
matter of fact, when I called, he raved about you. He told me you
were an impressive, extremely focused individual. He also said you
were probably operating two or three levels above your paygrade.
He admired how you could shut everything out and just focus on
a problem until it was solved. It's kind of funny actually, but from
everything he told me, it sort of reminded me of . . . well, me."

Sara's mouth fell open. "You can't be serious."

"I was all about the science, just like you seem to be. Your talent
and dedication are a potent combination. But why do you want to
make the move to our company and why this position? Why do
you want to be a lab supervisor?"

*Okay. You rehearsed this answer a million times. Just say the words.*

"Endosystems *is* a good place to work. And, they have treated
me well. I love it up North. But I've been there for three years and I
feel like it's time for a change. No one above me is going anywhere
soon and I'm ready to start directing the research, rather than just
carrying it out. As your lab supervisor, I think you'll find I'm not
only responsive to this company's goals but also will take the initiative in seeing others are, as well. Precision and results are of
supreme importance to me and I will make every effort to ensure

Techular's research objectives are reached efficiently and effective-ly."

Raj said nothing. Absolutely nada. *What is this all about? Did I say something wrong? Something stupid?*

"Okay," he finally said. "So, why this position?"

*Is he kidding?* "Dr. Patel—"

"Please, call me Raj."

"Oh. Uh, Raj . . . well, Techular has become one of the most re-spected biotech companies in the world, thanks to your work. I can only imagine what you're tackling next. Who wouldn't be excited and honored to be a part of it!"

"We are taking on some new things, that much I can say. The details are confidential, of course. But, you're on target there."

*He left the end of that sentence hanging in the air. What's coming next?* Her hands were sweating again. *He said he liked my work. I got a great reference. Stay calm, Sara. You can do this.*

"As I said, your credentials are outstanding. You're clearly moti-vated. Your work is beyond reproach. But let me say a few things back to you that I'm hearing, and, please correct me if I'm wrong."

"Um, sure."

"You're a scientist. You like the hands-on aspect. You love re-search. You're excited to discover new things. That's why you want to work here."

"Yes, yes. All that is true," she said, unsure where the disconnect was coming from.

"But this is a leadership position."

"Of course," she blurted out. "I know that and I'm ready for the responsibility."

"Well, the thing is, every step you take up the ladder leads away from the science. Toward people."

"Okay . . ."

*Okay? That's no way to respond! Oh no, I'm going to mess this up.*

"I can see my words are just starting to sink in. As we discussed a minute ago, you're used to burying your head in *your work*. For you, it's all-consuming. Am I right?"

"Yes, but I promise I would bring this same level of dedication to my team."

Raj laughed. "I see. Like I said, you remind me of me."

"I'm beginning to feel like that isn't a good thing?"

Raj leaned forward. "It is and isn't. From this moment on, let go of your mission to prove your competence and drive as a scientist. That isn't what this interview is about. You don't have to prove yourself to me on those grounds. We've already confirmed that. You don't even have to prove that we should want you on our team. Congratulations, we do!"

Sara was confused. Raj continued, "Now, the question for me is, what is the best and highest use of your talents? Do you want to do the work or lead the people?"

"Well, um, first, thank you." *Collect yourself, Sara.* "To answer your question, I see the next step as taking charge of a larger team of researchers and assistants to broaden my impact and pursue opportunities I see but others ignore. I have always prided myself on working well with people when required and treating them with respect."

"Good, that is good. But working *with* people is one thing. *Leading* them is another. You must be able to stop doing some of your old work and spend a substantive amount of time on the people. To be an effective leader, you must be willing to turn a group of scientists into a formidable community of effort . . . and, that is not easy. *We* are not easy. Sara, I know you're an excellent scientist. But what I am asking is, are you ready to jeopardize your focus on science by introducing a new discipline into the mix? Are you ready to be a leader? Is this even something you want?"

Sara was unprepared for this line of questioning. "I'm sorry. I'm confused. I don't understand. I thought this was a research position in the lab." She motioned to the lab beyond the window. "I get what you're saying about tending to the people but really, the people are there to *do* the science, right? How is that a step away? I mean, won't my job be to oversee the research, develop the methods, run experiments, etcetera?"

"Almost."

"Almost?"

"Your boss, the manager of lab and research operations, will be holding you accountable for developing a team whose capabilities exceeds the skill of any single member, including you."

Sara's anxiety was growing. She could feel her dream slipping. "I want this job and I don't mean to be a contrarian; I just don't think that's a fair expectation."

"Good. Please be candid. It's essential." Raj smiled.

Sara took a deep breath, trying to overcome her fear and frustration.

Raj began again. "Don't worry. I will not hold your candor against you. Quite the opposite. I will hold you to it. There is no trick here. You're hired. The question is, for what position? And, the best part is, you get to choose. But first, I want to make sure you know what you're getting into. I want to challenge you to think about what it means to lead. I want to make sure you have considered how it will change your daily work, how it will change your life and the lives of others."

"Yes, of course. I know it's a leadership position and I am prepared to—"

Raj held up his hand. He kept making her feel like she was somehow screwing up this interview. Yet, he didn't seem angry.

"Look out there." Raj pointed to the lab. "Every one of them is a gifted scientist. We wouldn't have it any other way. But why do we need them if you are more capable alone than they are together? Would they stay or would they leave, like you are leaving Endosystems? Who would be next in line after your next promotion? Would we succeed with our current research objectives? What about tomorrow's? Sara, leading is not about being the best and the smartest person in the room. It's about harnessing the collective power of all the souls in the room, finding more if you need them, and achieving things together as a community you could not do alone."

"I have to be honest. I haven't had a lot of experience with the kind of team you're talking about. None of my previous bosses cared about the team, some of them had favorites to whom they gave the more interesting and complicated work. But we weren't a team. We certainly weren't a community," Sara instantly regretted her tone.

"Of course. Regrettably, this is how most of us have operated. For years. And, it's exactly why I interview every potential leader. I want to be sure they understand what the job is *here*. And I want you to know the standard we will be holding you to, should you choose to accept."

Sara felt uncomfortable. Her anxiety had turned to frustration. "Dr. Patel, I really want this job. But I don't want to let you down. I thought this was exactly what I wanted. But to be honest, for most of my life I have used science to succeed without having to rely on the ups and downs of other people and their emotions. I feel safer when it's just me and the work. I feel awful for wasting your time. I guess you were wrong, I'm not like you . . . not really."

"Ha! You're right."

Sara's heart sank at the force of Raj's statement. He seemed excited by her defeat. *I'm going to be sick. How can he be so callous? I need to get out of this room.*

"You are definitely right. But not for the reason you think. Hear me out. Please. Do not despair. Sit proudly, the main difference between us is how quickly and easily you came to a place of true humility and self-awareness . . . whereas I took more than 40 years!"

Sara stared blankly at Raj.

"Look at this." Raj grabbed a picture on his desk and handed it to Sara. She observed a friendly-looking, well-dressed man she didn't recognize beside another man who looked vaguely familiar. *Is that Raj? Wow! This is a very different Raj than the one behind the desk today. This Raj looks like he doesn't own a comb—or a razor. His lab coat is a mess. And, he is noticeably heavier.*

"Is this you?" She asked sheepishly.

"That's me, all right. The man next to me is Mak Reddy. He co-founded this company with me and Franky. He was a scientist, too. But truthfully, not a great one. He was the best friend I ever had. One of my only friends back then. You see, I was the opposite of a leader. I did the science and he managed people. The arrangement worked well until about six years ago, when he died after a horrible accident."

"Wait. I think I heard about this. You were there, right? How terrible."

"Yes, I was there. It happened in front of the entire management team. It was truly, truly awful. I lost my best friend. And, for a while, this company lost its way."

"Is that when you became a leader? Because you had to?"

"I became a leader that day but didn't *start* leading until much later. When Mak died, the company spun out of control. I hid in the lab even though I had accepted the CEO role. Then our silent partner started being, well, not so silent. Eventually, she went around my back to have me fired—as CEO at least."

"That's awful," Sara gasped.

"Yes, it's still a source of embarrassment."

"No, I mean that she went around your back." Sara clarified, worried Raj though she meant he was awful.

"Yes, well, I left her no choice. After a while, I realized I wasn't betrayed. I was the betrayer. I had left the company and its people twisting in the wind. And, I had to change."

"Wow." Sara didn't know what else to say. Then she blurted out, "How?"

"The details are for another discussion. But I credit Franky for getting through to me. She had tried just about everything. I was a lost cause. And then suddenly, something changed. *We changed.* We started partnering and talking about what leading really is and how to do it. It's been a long road from that day to this one. And, I have taken more steps away from the work than I ever imagined. And, somehow, just as Franky promised me, with every step I took backward, the team accomplished more! And so I took another . . . and another. The bigger the gap I created; the more talented individuals flocked in to fill it!"

"That's an incredible journey." Sara was genuinely feeling inspired. She understood the point Raj was making even though the thought of relying on others to fill the gap unnerved her. It was hard to imagine going through a transformation like this herself.

*Maybe he sees something in me. Maybe he thinks I can do this? Would he even trust me if I changed my mind?*

Sara put the photo back on Raj's desk. She hadn't realized she was still holding it. Raj moved it back into place. As he did, he smiled. "Now, back when I started this journey, the idea of having to truly engage with and trust others scared me . . . a lot."

She nodded. *He sees me. I guess we really are alike.*

"But, let me tell you something. If I've learned anything, it's this: you have to know what the job actually is, and you have to want to do it. That's why I do these interviews. I believe—scratch that, I *know* if you're open to growing in this direction, you will excel at it. But I don't want you to think it's your only choice. I have taken great pains to develop a career path for senior scientists who are not interested in leading. Just say the word and we will find the right opportunity for you."

Sara didn't know how to respond. Before she knew it, the silence stretched beyond what was appropriate. She just couldn't find the words. Then, finally, she spoke. "This . . . this isn't the conversation I was expecting."

Raj chuckled. "And I'm sure you weren't expecting to have it with me, either."

"That's for sure."

"I wouldn't take the time if I didn't think you were worth it. Look, there are plenty of places that will just plunk you down in a position and not expect you to really lead. That's fine if you want to go in that direction, but I have to tell you, you'll be shortchanging yourself if you settle for less. I'm speaking from experience. If you truly want to do something great in this world, you must do it with others."

*I don't want to let him down. I don't want to let this company down. I just don't know if I'm capable of becoming what he wants me to be.*

"I should think about this. If there's time for me to do that?"

Raj didn't look offended. "Of course. Here's what you should do. Keep your follow-up interview with Evan. You two can chat as if this conversation never happened. If that meeting goes well, go home and think about the choice I'm presenting. We have plenty of room for someone of your talents. But we don't put or keep people in leadership positions who aren't willing to make leading their job. How does that sound?"

"Deal," she said.

| | | | |

The talk with Raj had done little to dissuade Sara from pursuing a position at Techular, but she was rattled to learn the position of her dreams was actually a nightmare. She had to swallow her fear. She had to try. That was why she was sitting across from Raj in this cute little tavern-style eatery exactly one week later.

When she had called, he had suggested lunch so they could talk outside the company walls in a more casual setting. She agreed readily. *I won't have any other people staring at me, wondering what I'm doing talking to the boss of the bosses again. If this doesn't work, no one else will ever know. I'll be safe.*

After receiving their iced teas and engaging in small talk, Sara began. "Dr. Patel—"

"Please, we are both doctors. Call me Raj."

"*Raj*, this is the job I want and the company I want to work for. I feel like this is where I'm supposed to be."

"Good, good," he said, perusing the menu.

"But I have to tell you. It scares the crap out of me." Sara instantly regretted using the word, *crap*. It felt too vulgar and too childish.

Raj looked up. "That's good."

"*It is?*"

"A real challenge should make you feel a little nervous. As I said, we all need to challenge ourselves once in a while to become better people."

"But the kind of leadership you're talking about . . . it's not natural to me. I can't promise I'll be any good at it at first."

"I appreciate your honesty. It's brave. And a good sign you're the kind of person we'd like to have at Techular. If you think back to our conversation, I think you will agree my focus wasn't on you being a natural leader. It was on understanding the responsibility and being willing to pursue it, to the detriment of hands-on work." Their server stopped by for their orders. When he was gone, Raj turned to Sara. "You say leading isn't natural to you. You heard my story when we spoke last week. Leading wasn't just a mystery to me, it was something I avoided like the plague."

"But you seem so comfortable with it now. Like it's second nature. I'd like to think that could be me but . . ."

Raj laughed. "Oh boy, if Franky were here, she'd be spitting out her iced tea. When we started, she thought I was hopeless!" Raj laughed. "If she hadn't kept at it, I don't know where I'd be today. Angry and alone, I suspect."

"What was the secret?"

"With Franky and me?"

"Yeah, what did she say that got your attention?".

"She changed the conversation. She started talking my language. She got specific. For the first time in my life, someone said, 'This is what leading is and this is how you do it.' Up until then, it all just sounded wishy washy and I never really knew what I was supposed to do or why."

"I just don't see how I could change my whole personality. I'm not mean to people but I definitely have trouble understanding them, their motives, all that stuff."

"Well, first things first, it's not about changing your personality. It's about building your own recipes for success. And then using and perfecting those recipes until they becomes second nature. Now, I hear what you're saying. It feels impossible. But, I was deep into my career when I began to take leading seriously. It changed my life—and more than just my work life. Now I enjoy paying it forward. If you're really committed to trying, I'll be there to help. All of us will be."

"I am committed. I don't do anything halfway."

Raj smiled, "I'm starting to pick up on that. We can kick things off right here at lunch . . . if you want."

"That would be excellent. It would help if I understood more about what you mean when you talk about recipes for leading. Oh darn, I wish I brought my notebook. I must have left it in the car."

"No need for a notebook quite yet. I promise we'll keep it simple for this discussion. I'll just focus on the three domains of leading and how we will tackle them, together."

The server arrived with their food: barbequed chicken sandwich for her, salad for Raj. When she left, Raj pointed at his iced tea.

"Okay, so when my mind tells my hand to pick up that glass, my hand does it, right?" He picked up the glass. "Most of the time, the body follows the mind." He took a sip.

*Where is this going?*

"But the thing is, the mind can also follow the body."

"I—I don't understand."

"There's an old Russian expression: 'Pretend to be a good person often enough and you will fool even God.' If you develop your own recipes for leading, what we call **LeadershipSOPs**, and use them again and again, you will increase your own aptitude and be in a position to continuously tweak them for better and better results. *Practice really does make perfect.* It also builds the *feel* you are missing today. The more you do something, the more *feel* you develop. And, as the positive reactions and results roll in, something magical will happen. You just can't help it. Your mindset and orientation toward the tasks will change. Being good at something just naturally does that. You will naturally begin to value leading. Then, one day you will wake to find yourself totally immersed in it."

"Maybe after like 20 years. Just kidding," she bit her lip. *Come on. A little less honesty. You going to make him retract the offer!* Sara sighed. "I mean . . . I am going to give it my all. I'm just worried I might not take to it like you did."

"You'd be surprised. I was as reclusive and reluctant as anyone could be. Without actually being a hermit."

"Really?"

"Really. Look, you and I are used to doing research based on scientific principles and sound lab procedures built around those principles. We don't have to go back and reread our procedures every time we design a new experiment, right? We *know* them because we put them to work every day. Can you remember a time when all the safety equipment you wear in the lab felt strange?" Raj paused long enough to see Sara nod, "Now, it feels weird when you don't have it on, doesn't it? It's like not wearing your seatbelt in a car. It doesn't feel right without it."

"True . . ."

"This is no different. You just have to be willing to engage in the work of leading. Even when it doesn't feel great. Give yourself permission to be a new leader, to get better as you go. The people who get themselves into trouble are those who pretend they are battle-hardened generals when they don't know what it is to be a corporal. The important thing is to build a strong leadership foundation. This means focusing on three key areas: structuring, operating, and perfecting your communities of effort."

*What does that even mean?* Sara broke eye contact, fearful Raj could tell she was already struggling to understand what he was saying.

"I get what you're thinking. What does that mean, really?"

Sara laughed, "How do you do that? It's like you're reading my mind."

"Perhaps now you will start believing when I tell you how much we are alike. Think about it this way. When you walk through the doors on your first day at Techular, you will be accountable for leading five or six employees. Your basic responsibilities will be to transform these individuals into a strong community of effort. To do this, you'll need to *structure* or organize the group, clarifying its purpose and objectives, ensuring they align up and across the organization, adjusting roles and responsibilities, stuff like that. You also will need to *operate* or manage it, helping to plan, assign, and monitor the work, hold the team accountable, engage critical stakeholders, etcetera. And lastly, you will need to *perfect* it, or seek out continual improvements, which includes coaching your employees and the team and engaging in performance improvement. We refer to these three areas as the three domains of leading. Mostly, you'll hear us talk about them as *structure, operate,* and *perfect* because the S, O, and P fit nicely with the **LeadershipSOPs** methodology I mentioned earlier."

"Oh, I see. So, SOPs stands for both standard operating procedures *and* structure, operate, and perfect. Tricky!"

"Yeah, we borrowed it from a guy named Lake Elliott. He was Franky's executive coach."

# LEADERSHIP SOPₛ

*Your standard operating procedures for structuring, operating, and perfecting your communities of effort.*

| STRUCTURE | OPERATE | PERFECT |
|:---:|:---:|:---:|
| *How, when and with whom do you organize?* | *How, when and with whom do you engage?* | *How, when and with whom do you improve?* |

# KEY QUESTIONS

- How does this community of effort (CoE) fit into its larger ecosystem?

- What is its core purpose?

- What are the long-term, midterm and short-term objectives?

- How would you describe the current and desired culture and what objectives would help close any gaps?

- What is the tactical plan to pursue the strategies and objectives?

- What are the cost implications and projected benefits of the tactical plan (i.e. budgeting process)?

- What mechanisms will be deployed to review plan execution and performance?

- How is work assigned?

- What mechanisms and processes are deployed to explore the need for individual, team and organizational development/improvement?

- What processes and tools help clarify potential obstacles and solutions for realizing development/improvement opportunities?

*continued*

| STRUCTURE | OPERATE | PERFECT |
|---|---|---|
| • What strategies should be deployed to pursue the objectives? | • Who will take part in the execution? | • How and when does development planning for individuals, teams and transformation initiatives occur? |
| • What are the right work methods and technologies? | • How will performance be monitored and evaluated? | |
| • How should this CoE be organized and governed? | • How will substandard performance be identified, communicated, and address? | • What coaching, mentoring and management processes and tools support individual, team and organizational transformation? |
| • What rewards systems are required to reinforce pursuing the business and cultural goals? | • What is the full list of internal and external stakeholders (customers, collaborators and competitors)? | • What methods and tools assist in the internalization and mastery of new behaviors and processes? |
| • What knowledge and capabilities are required to pursue the strategies and perform the work? | • By what means and under what schedule will they be engaged? | |

"Franky had a coach? I thought you said she was a natural leader."

"She sure did. And she is a natural. She definitely is. She actually brought him in to fix me, but he convinced her it would be more valuable for the two of us—Franky and me—to work things out together—so he coached her on how to reach me. You see, Franky's problem was the flips side of ours. She has always been a people person and a natural leader."

"I don't get it. How's that a problem? Why did she need a coach then?"

"Because you can't teach someone else your *gut* or your *feel*. In her case, she was born with a predisposition toward people and she even got better at it with time. In my case, it took a few million repetitions to take hold. Before her work with Lake, Franky would get frustrated with me and say things like, 'Engage your team more. Don't do everything yourself. Communicate with your peers, etcetera' and I just didn't know what to do with that. Then one day she said, 'Raj, the purpose of leading is to cultivate a powerful community of effort. And, since that's the case, you have to continually structure, operate, and perfect it. Now, let's work together and build your **LeadershipSOPs** to do it. . .' and bang, my world started to change."

"Seriously, it was that easy?" Sara's eyes widened with fear.

"Of course." Raj paused for effect. "No, no, no," Raj said, laughing. "I am just teasing. Like I said, I gave her a hard time every step of the way. But, as I look back over it all, that was the day the conversation changed."

Sara exhaled relief. "Oh, I was beginning to worry. Not because what you are saying doesn't make sense to me, but because I am still not really clear on what to actually do . . . the leading part I mean."

"Let's start with one concrete example that will apply to one of the most important things you will do with your team in the first few months."

Sara perked up, sensing they were finally going to talk about something she could get her arms around. "I know you said I wouldn't need to, but would you mind if I tapped a few notes into my phone? The ideas you're are sharing are simple but my mind is racing with things I need to do to put it into action."

"Of course, but once we get you set up on our systems, I'm going to send you a link to *LeaderForce*, which has a bunch of videos and easy-to-read information on all this stuff. In the meantime, you can just go to the **LeadershipSOPs** website—the concept has really grown over the years. You'll find a ton of stuff there."

"That would be great. What's, um, *LeaderForce*, though?" Sara asked, afraid she missed something.

"It's a digital leadership platform designed specifically for use with the **LeadershipSOPs**. You'll love it. We use it to document, trigger, and share our **LeadershipSOPs** and manage our communities of effort. It's a great resource for information and ideas."

"Nice. I will definitely be spending some time on it." The idea of a system to help her document and even trigger her new habits appealed to her.

"Anyhow, my point is that you can take notes if you want but it's more important for you to chew on the information a bit before worrying about memorizing *our* words or *our* models. In fact, we don't care if you ever repeat or remember a single one of our **LeadershipSOPs** acronyms."

"You don't?" Now Sara was really confused. "But I thought you . . ."

"What we care about most is leading. We use this framework because it's simple, memorable, and actionable. Please feel free to replace our words with yours at any time. It's the consistent behaviors that are nonnegotiable. Well, that's the official line anyway. There has been a huge benefit to our leaders all using the same basic methods *and* vocabulary. It's really improved our leadership culture and our employee engagement. You'll see when you go on

*LeaderForce* and look at the best practice templates and tools. So, I guess what I am saying is, while there is absolutely no requirement to memorize these words and concepts, you will definitely feel some cultural pressure to play along at times, or at the very least to speak the language when it's spoken to you. Does that make sense?"

"Absolutely but you won't get any argument from me. I'll need all the help I can get."

"Speaking of help, let me just introduce this one last topic and we can call it a day." Raj took a look at his watch. "Good. I have just enough time. Let's talk about scope. Your team will have a relatively small slice of your department's larger scope and your department's scope is just one component of our company's entire scope," Raj paused. "Do you see what I am saying?"

"Yes, of course, I think all organizations are like this, really. The company has a very broad scope and then it gets divided up by the organization's departments, which in turn divide up the work amongst their teams. Right?"

"Yes! In fact, I think you said that much better than I did. Now, keep that thought in your mind and allow me to deepen your definition of the word **SCOPE**. For us, it is another acronym. It stands for Strategy, Culture, Objectives, Purpose, and Ecosystem."

Raj continued, "Taken together, these five items define the basic architecture of any community of effort. Therefore, anytime we do strategic planning for a large or small group, we start at the 'E' and move toward the 'S.' In other words, we begin by defining the relevant ecosystem of stakeholder groups, starting with the easy ones, like customers, collaborators, and competitors, then add in the more complex ones we might have missed. For example, regulators and payors such as Medicare or private insurance companies, entities that aren't on the tips of our tongues when we think of the patients we are trying to help. Can you see how it's important to understand this ecosystem and the interactions within it?"

# SCOPE

*The **SCOPE** model helps leaders facilitate strategic planning and summarize the business architecture of a community of effort. More robust than the traditional "mission, vision, and values" components still used by many, **SCOPE** includes these elements but starts with a holistic review of the context (or ecosystem), considers the core purpose within the ecosystem, identifies long-term and short-term objectives, contemplates the current and desired culture, and results in strategies that inform resource deployment and action toward the primary business and cultural objectives.*

Sara nodded and added, "Sure, I mean I haven't really talked about it like this before, but I think it's why we value people with experience in our segment. Because they get it. They understand these interactions already. They understand our context."

"Perfect. Yes, you've got it. Now, as we are aligning on the eco-system and the primary interactions in it, we are also starting to determine how the group in question will add value to this eco-system. This is essentially how we define the community's purpose. Once we have clarified or created its purpose, we determine the long-term vision by asking ourselves what we are really trying to accomplish if we were successful beyond our wildest dreams. Then we take that big objective—what some people call 'vision'—and bring it forward, beginning with about three years out and ending with quarterly objectives for the current year. Next, as a last step before devising our strategies, we consider culture—both the culture we have and the culture we would like to have. How will the existing culture accelerate or hinder our success? Are the patterns of thinking, speaking, and acting we see in the group aligned with our vision of how we ought to be? This is a critical discussion which often informs the creation of new cultural objectives, and impacts the ultimate strategies we craft. The last thing we do is take all this information and ensure every objective has at least one strategy associated with it. Cultural and business objectives don't get achieved just because you write them down. They must be translated into action across the enterprise. But that doesn't happen easily because raw objectives don't indicate how people need to coordinate their behavior to achieve those objectives. To help explain our intent, we align on and communicate high-level themes to guide resource deployment and actions across the company. These themes are what we call strategies."

"Okay, I think I get it. I'm guessing where **SCOPE** leaves off is where tactical planning begins?" Sara asked, hopeful she was putting it all together.

"Exactly," Raj reassured her. "Between those two things, or at the very least, in tandem with the tactical planning, lies the determination of the organization you need to deliver the **SCOPE** and the operational plan."

"Okay, that makes sense. I mean, you need to have an organization that is capable of delivering its **SCOPE**. But, wow, this sounds like a lot of work. I see why it's so important, but I thought I was taking over a team that already existed. Wouldn't it already have a **SCOPE**?"

"Good question, it will be your job to engage the team and figure that out. You can't just get on the bus and assume it's going in the right direction. Just for the sake of argument, for the moment, let's pretend they do have a **SCOPE**. Do you suppose Techular's **SCOPE** is the same now as it was more than a decade ago when we started the company? Do you think it's even the same as it was last year?"

"Well, in my interview, you said you can't talk about the details, but it seems pretty clear Techular is going to be more than a one drug, one indication company. My guess is you either want to expand the use of the current treatment for something other than Alzheimer's and/or develop other treatments." Sara paused. Her face went blank as she thought over the implication of her answer. "Okay, I follow what you mean, I think. But it all just got way more complicated than I was initially thinking."

"Right!" Raj's face lit up with excitement. "Because . . . if the organization redefines even one component of its **SCOPE**, like its ecosystem, for instance, in the case of pursuing a new customer segment, that could create a lot of downstream havoc across the organization, right? For example, let's say we are talking about a biotech company, not ours, but a lot like ours." Raj shot her a look suggesting he did mean Techular but wasn't ready to say that just yet. "Maybe this company thrived as a result of delivering just one drug with just one approved indication or use to just one patient population. Now, what would happen if they wanted to gear up for new treatments or new uses affecting an entirely different patient population? The entire organization would have to revisit its purpose! New objectives would need to be developed. The culture would need to be evaluated in light of the objectives to determine the best, most effective strategies. And, all this work might result in the creation of entirely new teams, maybe even new departments."

"Whoa." Sara's brain was on fire thinking about the dominos falling across the organization. "And then, I suppose every department would have to reconstruct its **SCOPE** in alignment with the others and each department's teams would have to go after that."

"Yes, yes! Now you're seeing it. I can tell. So, this very thing is happening inside our organization to some extent all of the time. Sometimes we pursue a change that just makes small tweaks to our **SCOPE** and sometimes we take on big, expansive changes that threaten to reconstitute every team and every department. This is why we need our leaders leading, not hiding away doing the work. They need to see and understand that these changes are happening and adjust in ways that keep them in collaboration, not competition, with other groups. Think of the consequences if every leader were just working away in the lab, assuming nothing was changing around them."

"They could be wasting everyone's time. Working on the wrong things."

"Yes," Raj shot Sara a huge smile. "Or, they could be doing the right things but in the wrong way or at the wrong time or competing with another team's resources."

Sara's thumbs were tapping away on her phone, frantically capturing a thought. After a few seconds, she looked up. "Sorry, I wanted to get this conversation down. I guess the point of this is one of my first **LeadershipSOPs** should be my recipe for assessing and developing my team's **SCOPE**. Right?"

"Yes, indeed. I thought you said you *weren't* a natural. Now, you tell me. How might you get that done? Picture yourself arriving at Techular on your first day, meeting with Evan, meeting your team. How do you think you might approach this important task? When would you start?"

"When? As soon as I am able! I mean, I need access to a lot of information that I can't get until I'm officially onboard. But I would start as soon as I can get a hold of the information."

Raj smiled again. This time looking more like the Cheshire Cat. "Good. Yes, you will need more information than you have today. But, tell me more about what the work of gathering it will look like. Where will it get done? What role will your supervisor, Evan, play? What about your team? Where will they be in all this?"

"Well, I'm assuming some of the information will need to come from Evan since he should know the company's **SCOPE** and his department's **SCOPE.** He will likely also know more about my team and where they are versus where he would like them to be. So, I guess some of the work will get done through meetings with him and some of the other stakeholders in my, my . . ." Sara looked down at her notes, "Ecosystem."

*Strategy . . . how the heck do you develop a strategy? Damn it, Raj. I'm a scientist not a business consultant.*

She looked back up at Raj, realizing her thoughts had gotten away from her. "Then, I will need to do some research on strategy development and maybe see some other **SCOPE** documents at Techular to make sure I get the right stuff in mine. Then, after that, I guess I will need to confirm I've got it right with Evan before I communicate it to my team."

"Okay, you are off to a good start. I think this would be a great step forward for you." Raj paused. "Would you be open to an idea or two?"

"Open to it? I was kind of hoping we could have started there," Sara laughed and Raj joined in.

"Fair enough. I like letting you put your thoughts together first, because I have learned—the hard way—it is far better to let other people think through their own plans rather than saddle them with mine. It is never a good thing to be stuck trying to implement a plan you don't really own, understand, or like. This has become one of my own **LeadershipSOPs**. It helps me fight against my impulse to jump in and do other peoples' work. Anyhow, I want you to know about this **LeadershipSOP** for three reasons. One, I know from experience that it helps you understand the concept better if you hear some examples. It makes it all more concrete. Two, when I use this **LeadershipSOP**, people sometimes tell me it feels like I am quizzing them and they are somehow trapped in a game show trying to uncover an answer I already know but won't tell them—which is, of course, not my intent. Does that make sense?"

"It does and I'm glad you said that because it is a little intimidating," Sara confessed. "But before I explode, could you tell me your actual feedback? The suspense is killing me!"

"Sure, sure. That is my third reason for sharing this **Leadership-SOP** with you. Given what I just said about the challenges in owning a plan someone else crafts without you, what execution risks might you encounter by waiting until the end of your process to engage your team?"

Sara had been looking down at her phone, ready to capture Raj's thoughts. She instantly knew this had been a test. Whether Raj said so or not, it was and she had failed. She needed to look back up at him and respond. She knew that . . . but the shame was so heavy she couldn't lift her head an inch.

*Despite all this time he's spent with me, I blew it, Why, why, why! Of course, I need to do it with my team! I'm never going to succeed at this. I should just quit before I'm fired. Someone like me should be running tests, not teams!*

# CHAPTER TEN

# THE

# JOKESTER

*What fresh hell is this?*

That's what Mark's weird old Aunt Esther used to say whenever she heard the doorbell ring. For some reason, it stuck in his brain. Now, whenever he was confronted with the unknown, he always asked himself the same question. This was one of those times. He and the rest of the research team were about to meet their new supervisor and they were all leery about it.

They already knew her name: Sara Chen. Through some basic Googling, Mark saw she had the requisite academic credentials and had done well for herself at Endosystems Engineering. But, as far as he could tell, she had never been in charge of anyone else. Plus, from the graduation dates, he suspected she was at least a year *younger*. It's not like he wanted the job, necessarily, but he didn't like the idea of someone younger bossing him around . . . or making more money. He wondered what Evan was smoking, bringing in this newbie—she would probably end up just like Jonathan.

"Any minute now," sighed Carolina. "Hey. Who cares? It's not as if we have any work to do."

Mark laughed. He liked Carolina. They shared the same snarky sense of humor. For the third time in the last minute he found himself glancing at the window of Raj's office. He could see Raj, Evan, and Sara still talking. *Why is Raj so involved with this one? Where is Katarina? She is Evan's boss, after all. Has there been some kind of shake-up? Is there going to be one?*

He turned his gaze back to his team. More than a few tense expressions peered back at him. Their last supervisor wasn't so much a jerk as he was just, indifferent. Mark kind of liked it at first, but then he started to resent Jonathan's lack of engagement, his unwillingness to make decisions or even recognize the work he and Carolina were doing. *This one had better give out spot bonuses. I'm sick of the other teams scooping up all the extra cash.*

"How long do you think this is going to last?" Carolina said to the group.

"You mean, if it ever starts? I'm thinking there will be at least 10 minutes of meaningless chatter. She's excited to be here . . . blah, blah, blah. She's looking forward to getting to know each of us . . . yada, yada, yada." Mark joked.

She laughed, then turned quiet. Clearly, Carolina wasn't looking forward to this, either. Nobody was. Everyone was getting uncomfortable. When Jonathan, their last supervisor, left for "another opportunity" after just six months, they knew what it really meant. He had been fired or quit after a bad performance review. Evidentially, Mark wasn't the only one who noticed Jonathan wasn't doing anything. Evan must have, too.

Even though it was warranted, Jonathan's firing had a chilling effect on the team—which is why they had to look outside to find candidates. Nobody wanted to get promoted over their peers and then find themselves fired and humiliated six months later.

In the interim, tensions had been building. Of course, things were getting done without a direct supervisor. Everyone knew their jobs well enough, but the real problem was Evan couldn't give them enough time for all the daily decisions that needed to be made. *How could he?* He had five other lab teams under him. This meant some of team members charged ahead while others hesitated, waiting for somebody's say so. Consequently, there had been more than one spat over the past month or so.

Sitting here now, Mark was surprised by the growing sense of regret he felt over not putting his own hat in the ring. He didn't like the feeling of an outsider stepping into the role. Who knows whose side she was going to take in the several little conflicts brewing. *It's ridiculous. Everybody here knows what's expected. Somebody just needs to stay on them to make sure they get the work done. I can't believe not a single one of us stepped up.*

"I see movement." Carolina said.

Mark saw Evan escorting Sara out of Raj's office and down the hall. "Here she comes. Ladies and gentlemen, welcome to your new hell." Everybody groaned as they usually did at his jokes, but he enjoyed irritating them. He laughed ruefully to himself. *Who says science has to be so serious?*

Aaron, a tense-looking research veteran who never aspired to anything except research, watched intently as Evan opened the door.

"Folks, please welcome Sara Chen, your new lab supervisor. She's super talented, super smart and finally done with all the paperwork and pep talks," Evan said. "I know you'll give her the same level of respect and support you did me."

"I would think you'd want better for her than that," quipped Mark.

Evan pointed to Mark as a smattering of laughter evaporated. "Watch out for that one, he's a jokester." Then he turned back to the group. "Well, I don't want to micromanage the introductions, so, without further ado . . ." He outstretched his arm, indicating Sara should step in front and do her little song and dance. As she did, he began his exit.

"Thanks Evan. I'll take it from here," said Sara as Evan waved goodbye.

Sara took a deep breath as she looked over the group. Mark

couldn't help thinking she looked like a shy preschooler at show-and-tell. *She's nervous. You can see it in her eyes. This could be another short-lived reign. Might be for the best.*

"So . . . hi, everybody," she said in an awkward way. "I'm Sara, but I guess we already established that, didn't we?"

A few polite chuckles. She definitely wasn't coming on strong. No, that wouldn't be her style, Mark could tell.

"Some of you . . . well, you actually look as nervous as I feel," she went on. "It reminds me of when they tell you not to worry about the wildlife . . ."

Blank stares. *She's dying up there. This is painful.*

". . . You know, they're more afraid of *you* than you are of *them*."

Sara waited for a laugh that never came. Mark and Carolina shared a skeptical look. *Aaaaand she's lost them.*

"I'm sorry. Was that weird?" Sara said, acknowledging the silence. "That felt weird."

"It's okay," Mark piped up. "We do well with weird." Mark was pleased when the group laughed with him this time.

"Okay, great. Then we'll all be fine, I guess!" Something about this last exchange seemed to make her feel more comfortable. It broke the ice, at least.

*Tension eased. The floor is yours.*

"So, let me 'reboot' my introduction," she said with more assurance. "And let's pretend I never said anything about you being analogous to wildlife . . . or that you were afraid . . . or that I was afraid." The team chuckled, seemingly enjoying her delivery. "Anyway, good morning. I'm excited to be here and I'm looking forward to this opportunity to work with you all."

Nobody moved. Or said a thing. Mark and several others stifled a laugh. *OMG, this is my speech, word for word. Well, without the yada, yadas.*

"So, it's not just my first day here. It's actually my first day as a supervisor, here or anywhere. Certainly, I'm no stranger to our work. But this is a new opportunity for me—one which I intend to take seriously. Anyhow, I've never been fond of the cliché, 'Never let 'em see you sweat.' One of my core personality traits is candor, and as you've no doubt noticed, my delivery is often a little awkward. So, if I'm sweating, I'm going to tell you I'm sweating. And, well, I'm sweating."

*Um yeah, we can tell. This is painful to watch.*

"But I want you to know it's not because of our work as scientists; I trust you'll find me a valuable thought partner when it comes to that. The truth is, I'm sweating because when I took this job I thought it was about two things: the science and my career. And now, as I look you all in the eyes, I can see what it's really about, the team . . . and I don't want to let you down. I am a bit handicapped in this area though, having spent more time with pipettes than people in the last 10 years."

*Um rousing speech, boss—where are you going with this?*

"I do know one thing about people, though. We are carbon-based life forms. And, as everyone here knows, there is no difference between the carbon that makes up graphite and diamonds. It's the strength of the bonds between the carbon molecules that makes one substance brittle and the other harder than steel. Today, my arrival is disruptive and unnerving. But my hope is that someday soon, the bonds we create between us will produce something special and rare, something that can cut through anything in our path."

For a brief second, there was silence. "Wow. That got deep," Mark said, filling the silent space. It stayed silent with several team members shooting Mark an uncomfortable look. *Too soon to start sniping? Maybe.*

Sara turned red but didn't skip a beat. "I guess Evan was right, I do need to watch out for you." The team joined in a round of laughter at Mark's expense.

Carolina laughed hardest. "He thinks he's funny . . . but, well, you can see what we've been dealing with."

"Hey, you're laughing aren't you?" Mark said, feigning insult.

"I was going to ask everyone to introduce themselves, so maybe you should go first?" Sara said, keeping her eyes on Mark.

"Sure. I'm Mark." He gave a little bow to her, then to the team. Aaron glared, as if thinking to himself, "Stop acting like a jackass."

*Is everyone losing their sense of humor?*

"Okay, Mark, maybe a little more detail?" Sara replied.

Mark nodded, allowing the room another laugh at his expense. *At me, with me, I don't care which.*

"I am one of three research leads . . ."

Sara interrupted him midsentence. "Actually, you know what, I have been studying everyone's bios for the last week, so I know the basics. Why don't you share something about yourself, maybe something that will help me and the team understand you better?"

"Wait, what? What do you mean?" Mark said with genuine confusion.

"For instance, I told you that I'm extremely candid, even when it might be a little strange. I didn't just tell you that because I was nervous. I wanted the team to know that sometimes I will find it hard to stop myself from putting uncomfortable things on the table . . . and I don't want it to be a surprise or have people thinking I am rude or angry."

"Um, yeah, I don't know. Pass?"

Sara didn't seem to miss a beat. Or look flustered. "Oh, don't give up so easily. Perhaps you could tell us why you joke around so much. We don't have a lot of class clowns in our line of work."

*How did this happen?* Mark definitely didn't see this coming. "Well, I, um, I have always felt like people take themselves too seriously. I think humor eases tension and loosens things up a bit. You know, instead of everyone being so uptight."

"Great. That might be helpful to the group. We can use you like a barometer to let us know when the pressure is building. But, just so I'm clear, when you start cracking jokes should I assume it's the whole team that's uncomfortable, or just you?"

Mark eyes went as wide as saucers. He was sure he had a good reply in his back pocket, but he couldn't figure out which one it was in before Carolina pounced, "Look out, Mark. She is on to you." The team erupted in laughter, including Mark.

Sara looked as if she was just realizing how her comment came across. "I'm sorry, Mark. I wasn't even trying to be funny."

"Um, yeah. I think that's what gave it the extra zing!" Mark said, laughing at the scenario. "We are going to get along just fine, Sara. Welcome to the team."

As everyone else took turns introducing—and laughing—at themselves, Mark watched Sara. She surprised him. Once she got over her initial jitters, she recovered nicely. She still seemed awkward, quirky even, but genuine and definitely *not* a pushover. The team seemed to like her, too. She even knew how to come back at him. *I'm not buying that excuse for one minute. She knew what she was doing . . . and I loved it.*

After the introductions, Sara looked the group over. "Thanks everyone, for indulging me. I know you're probably itching to get back to the lab, but I would like to talk about the next 30 days."

*Here it comes. Just when I was starting to like her.*

"I need to establish a bunch of recurring meetings." A few people huffed. "I know. I know. Nobody likes to waste time in meetings. My promise is we will only have them for as long and as frequently as we need them. Eventually, we can all decide that together. For now, I need to establish a weekly cadence to ensure the communication lines are open. Additionally, I will be setting up a series of one-on-ones with each of you to make sure I understand the current flow of work across the team: your strengths, career goals, etcetera. At the same time, I will be meeting with the leaders of our sister teams in Evan's department. I want to make sure we are well positioned to deliver our portion of the department's **SCOPE.**"

Mark put up his hand. "Okay, I have a question. And it's not a joke."

"Sure, Mark."

"What do you mean by 'positioned?'" Mark's words hung in the air.

"Well, as you know, the organization has been going through a lot of changes and I want to make sure we have the right operating model and structure to hit our portion of the department's objectives."

"Wait a minute. Are you saying you're not sure if we can do our jobs?" Mark didn't mean to be so biting with his words, but he was getting concerned.

"Oh, no. Of course not! Sorry, I didn't mean to imply that at all. I just want to make sure our efforts—as a team—are in the right direction, given all the changes in Evan's department and across the company. And, I want us to do that together. I'm going to collect some information across the next four weeks and then next month, we are going to pull ourselves out of the lab for a day and see what we think the information is telling us."

"Wait, what changes? Are you sure? I don't think we have the time for a whole day. Have you seen our schedule?" It was the first thing Aaron had said for awhile . . . and even he looked surprised he said it.

"I know. It is a lot of time out of the lab, but solid planning is absolutely essential to ensuring every minute of work on the floor is valuable to Evan and the company as a whole."

It was Carolina who piped up this time. "So were you brought in here to do this? I mean, does Evan think we're on the wrong track? Are we thinking about outsourcing research and development or something? Because . . ."

"Okay, okay, I want everyone to relax." Sara interrupted. "Mark, tell a joke or something." Sara paused for a round of nervous laughter. "I don't think we should assume anything one way or the other. There have been a lot of changes across the organization and I don't have a good sense of how they have or haven't been incorporated." The team was completely silent. Sara continued, "When was the last time you did any planning, as a group?"

"Um, never." Said Li.

"What? Never?" Sara was shocked given her introduction to the company and all the talk about **LeadershipSOPs** and **SCOPE**, etcetera.

"Yeah, I mean, this team was established six months ago when Jonathan was hired. Prior to that, we were all on different teams." Li elaborated.

"Except for me." Horik said. "Jonathan hired me about a month or so after he got here. I, for one, would be interested in doing some planning. It might resolve some of the debates we've been having."

Mark piped up again. "So seriously, should we be worried? What are these changes you keep talking about?"

"Honestly Mark, I think we should be more worried that we're currently navigating without a compass. My guess is we shouldn't be too concerned because Evan was leaning in while he conducted the search for my role and he didn't mention any specific concerns. I think the **SCOPE**-ing session will be a great opportunity for us to talk about the value we bring to Techular and how we want to work together to deliver that value. This isn't a case of the company making us change—the company already has changed. This planning process is just us deciding how to best adjust to it."

"Again, what change," exclaimed Mark, feeling exasperated. He looked around, realizing he needed to dial things back a bit. "Sorry. I didn't mean to get so excited. And, I'm not trying to be sarcastic. I really don't know what you mean by changes."

Several other members of the team nodded in agreement.

"Oh, really? Um, okay, let's walk through it for just a second.

Moments after I signed my nondisclosure agreement, I was informed of what I assume you all knew already. Techular Biologics does not want to be a one drug, one treatment company. And it is making some serious investments, likely in the tens of millions of dollars, during the next year or so to retool the entire organization and deliver on this vision. During my onboarding discussions with Raj, he shared his belief that this would ultimately impact every function, every research team in the company. He is excited to see the organization expand and I think we should be excited, too. It's much easier to do research when a group is expanding versus contracting." Sara looked around, noticed her team's faces had changed. "What did I say? Mark, help me out here."

Mark just scrunched up his face. Then Horik chipped in to break the silence. "Well, I can't speak for the others, but I didn't really get the same message you just delivered. There was an email a while back from Raj and Franky, but we missed the last Lab Operations All Hands Meeting last quarter because Jonathan had us rerunning priority tests."

"I heard the investment part." Carolina added. "From a colleague on one of the other teams. She came back from the All Hands excited about it. I didn't realize it impacted us, though. Jonathan never said anything. It sounded like a good thing, so I just left it at that."

"Wow, I'm so sorry. I feel like we need to do this whole meeting over. Seriously, I feel like I totally didn't know what I was walking into."

"That makes seven of us!" Mark exclaimed as the room erupted into more nervous laughter.

"No, I am dead serious. I want a total do-over!" Sara shut her eyes and raised both hands out in front of her as if she were holding back the real world from making it into the new altered reality she was formulating in her mind. The team traded looks. Several people quietly laughed to themselves, trying to keep as quiet as possible to refrain from embarrassing their new boss.

Sara drew in a long, noisy breath of air, then let it back out again. "Sara Chen introduction take three." Suddenly, her eyes burst wide open. Good morning team, I am Sara, Sara Chen and I'm your new leader. I am excited to work with each of you. My understanding is that this team has been somewhat isolated from all the exciting changes going on across the organization."

*Seriously, are we really going to do this?* Mark looked around the room. Everyone else seemed as amazed as he was.

Sara continued despite the group's hesitancy. "As a result, our first priority will be to engage in a collaborative effort to explore the expanding **SCOPE** of Techular Biologics—that's scope as in S.C.O.P.E. It stands for Strategy, Culture, Objectives, Purpose, and Ecosystem. As we reexamine the company's new **SCOPE**, we will need to look at our smaller *ecosystem* as just one of the labs in this department and determine if our *purpose* within it has changed. We will need to understand what new long-term and short-term *objectives* need to be established and determine how these changes might be supported or challenged by our historical *culture*. Does our culture need to change or be preserved? Then, we will need to take a look at all of this new information and see what new *strategies* might be required for deploying resources and informing action toward our objectives.

"I expect this journey to be both difficult and rewarding. Difficult because change itself is never easy. Rewarding because I know the process will grow us as professionals and as a team. However alarming on its face, I do suspect this discussion to alter how we define our core work and how we go about it. I think it will impact our structure by changing how we think about our roles and responsibilities and the basic mix of knowledge and capabilities we require as a team. More than that, I think it will change when and how frequently we plan; how we assign, execute, monitor, and evaluate the work we do. It will change what other groups we engage; how we engage each other; how we hold ourselves and the team accountable. And . . . here's the really important part, we won't get it right! Not the first time or even the second. We'll have to be honest with one another as a team and keep making changes. Eventually, we need to build enough trust and shared ownership across this team that every single one of *my* **LeadershipSOPs** gets turned into *our* **MembershipSOPs**."

Sara had stopped talking in the middle of what seemed like an important thought. It seemed like there was supposed to be more, but she just stopped dead. There was complete silence. Mark looked at her and tilted his head sideways. *Are you done?*

"Tah-dah!" Sara shouted, throwing out her arms to better signal the official completion of her speech.

The silence stretched out for another beat.

It was Horik that finally broke it. "Perfect. Bravo!" He said with a clap. He was immediately joined by the others.

"I love it," said Aaron as Sara took a seated bow, a bit red with embarrassment.

Mark was . . . amazed by the strange balancing act she achieved. It was clear she didn't like the attention, but had found an odd sense of humble strength and clarity. She looked transformed by her own words, as if the speech was really for her instead of them. It was hard not to enjoy it with her.

*Don't make me like you, Sara Chen.*

"Wait, what did you do with our nervous, first-time manager? Someone call the FBI! Sara's been abducted by aliens . . . or worse . . . executives!" Mark exclaimed, taking a stab at re-establishing himself as the team jokester.

As the laughing died down, Sara said, "I know we can do this. We will figure it out together. Honestly, Mark's right, I was *super-duper* nervous when I walked in here, but it was because I wasn't sure

# LEADERSHIP SOP<sub>s</sub>

*Your standard operating procedures for structuring, operating, and perfecting your communities of effort.*

| STRUCTURE | OPERATE | PERFECT |
|---|---|---|
| *SCOPE the WORK* | *Set the PASE* | *Transform & Master* |

### SCOPE

Every community of effort has a SCOPE. It represents the primary business architecture of the group. Reaching beyond mission, vision and values, SCOPE stands for: strategy, culture, objectives, purpose, and ecosystem.

### WORK

The WORK acronym comprises the second half of the LeadershipSOPs organizational design model, alluding to the work methods, organizational structures, rewards and recognition, knowledge and capabilities required to pursue and deliver the SCOPE.

### PASE

The PASE model includes planning (operational and financial), accountability, and stakeholder engagement. Frequently, these operational dimensions account for the bulk of a leader's time.

### AEMEA
### Accountability Model

The AEMEA accountability model breaks down the "A" in PASE into the critical components of a work execution system with each letter referring to the assignment processes; execution planning; monitoring mechanisms; evaluation routines; and actions required to manage performance.

### ECT(M)

Personal transformation and change leadership are hard. Most (66% or more) change initiatives result in failure. ECT(M) is an individual coaching, team development and organizational transformation model which actively engages those seeking or impacted by change in the proactive phases of what is known as the change curve. The model focuses on cycling through the explore, clarify, and transform phases multiple times until success is ultimately found. Then, the pursuit of mastery begins by integrating the change into new standard operating procedures.

how to add value as a leader, versus a scientist. But now, I see it. I see how I can help."

The team got up, heading for the door. Each stopped to shake Sara's hand on the way out. Mark maneuvered himself to the end of the line. "Great job boss," he said, shaking her hand. "Weird . . . but great."

| | | | |

*Okay, say it right away. Then you're on the hook and you have to fol-low-though this time.*

"Hey, what's up?" Sara said, noticing Mark hovering outside her discussion with Li.

"I'm sorry for cutting in. I just wanted to . . . could I have a sec-ond when you and Li are finished?" Mark said awkwardly.

"We're actually done here." Sara looked back at Li to confirm.

Li nodded her head in agreement. "I got what I needed. Thanks."

"So, what can I do for you sir?" Sara asked.

"Could we do this off the floor? It's kind of private." Mark mo-tioned to the wide-open space of the lab.

Sara looked surprised to hear Mark considered any of his thoughts private. "Yeah, let's grab a privacy room." The two walked out the double doors, stepping into a small conference room de-signed for personal calls and impromptu meetings. As Mark sat down, she stretched her hand outside the room and changed the sign to read, "occupied." Then she shut the door and took on a very concerned tone, "Everything okay? You don't seem yourself."

*Here it goes.* "I need your help getting off this team."

Sara pulled her head back in surprise. "What?"

Mark took a deep breath. "Ever since your first day, I've been get-ting madder and madder. And I just can't take it anymore. It should have been me . . . or, at least I should have put my hat in the ring."

Sara sank in her chair, clearly disappointed. "Mark, I don't know what to say. I thought we were working well to—"

Mark cut her. "Sorry. You don't understand. I don't mean there is anything wrong with you or the team. Ugh, I kind of messed this up."

"No worries. Take a do-over. I do it all the time."

"I didn't apply for your position because I was afraid whomever took the role would be gobbled up and humiliated. But look at you. It's been almost a year and you're doing great . . . *we're doing great.* And you didn't do it with some iron first or magic dust. You just installed a bunch of common-sense systems and put us back on track. I could have—and should have had the courage to stick my neck out. Every day I come in here now and regret it more and more. I am not angry with you. I am angry with myself."

"Jeez. Why didn't you just say so, Mark? That's what our one-on-ones are for. To discuss this kind of stuff."

"I know, but I keep on avoiding it or cracking jokes instead of hitting it head-on. Then, yesterday, I got an alert saying there was an opening for a lab supervisor. I pulled everything together last night to put in for it and then two things stopped me cold."

"Really? It seems like you're mentally ready."

"The first thing that hit me was a feeling of betrayal. I knew if I hit that button, word could get to you before I did . . . and that just didn't feel right."

Sara shot him a half-smile. "Ah shucks. Thanks, you old softy. Now, what was the real reason?"

Mark smirked, "The second was the interview with Raj. I suddenly remembered you saying he interviews all incoming leaders and I have to tell you I am more than a little scared to sit in front of him and tell him I'm ready for this. The only reason he even knows me is because of my jokes. He probably thinks I am the class clown. Not real leadership material. Then, that made me think of Evan. Before I even got to Raj, I would have to go through Evan. And, Evan doesn't *think* I'm a jokester. He *knows* I am. Sara, what am I going to do?"

"Mark, I can't change who you are."

"So, you're not gonna help me?" Mark's face showed his shock and horror.

"What? No, of course, I'll help you, you dingbat! But I'm not going to help you by changing who you are. We'll start by reviewing the **SOPs** of leading and making sure you really understand and want the job. I mean, Raj has seen to it that there are a lot of other ways to expand your influence and get a raise around here than just leading people. But, if you really want to take your first step away from the science and toward leading people, we can discuss how to build your own **LeadershipSOPs** to drive an effective leadership style that's all your own . . . because nerdy and quirky have already been taken!" Sara gave him a cheesy wink that Mark barely noticed.

He was too deep in thought. *Away from the science . . . ?*

# ABOUT THE AUTHOR

 Edward E. Tyson is the chief executive officer of PerSynergy Consulting. He is a former strategy executive and Marine turned executive coach and organizational consultant. As the architect of the **LeadershipSOPs,** a ground-breaking leadership framework and methodology, Ed encourages leaders to develop and deploy personal standard operating procedures for structuring, operating, and perfecting their communities of effort. Challenging convention, this simple but robust model promotes engaging in the actual work of leading *before* developing interpersonal skills and styles, believing the reverse (putting soft skills first) results in fruitless attempts to bridge critical hard skills' gaps with soft skills aimed at the *how*, instead of the *what*.

Before founding PerSynergy in 2013, Ed accumulated 20 years of leadership experience in a range of military, non-profit, private, and publicly traded organizations. Ed joined the United States Marines at the age of 17 and received a bachelor's degree in philosophy from Pennsylvania State University. After college, Ed attended Temple University while working as the director of education for the Pennsylvania Health Care Association, earning a master's degree in adult organizational development. During his professional career, he held executive positions in process improvement and strategy development and led functional areas as varied as spend management and corporate marketing. Since making the move to external consulting, his experience has been just as diverse, working across the energy, medical devices, legal services, biotech, big tech, and professional services sectors (to name just a few).

A master facilitator and speaker, Ed has worked hand-in-hand with boards, leadership teams, and C-level leaders around the country to assess and solve issues ranging from solvency to strategy. He is a tested executive coach and team development expert. As both an internal executive and an external consultant, he has led multimillion-dollar change initiatives impacting tens of thousands, developed strategic plans for companies of all sizes and sophistication, and completed scores of strategic reorganizations.

Ultimately, Ed attributes much of his success to his ability to deconstruct and simplify complex issues, think quickly but react calmly, and reframe even the toughest of discussions. Stylistically, he brings a unique blend of positive energy, calm intensity, and humor to serious discussions requiring rapid resolution.